The WITCH
And WIZARD
TRAINING GUIDE

The WITCH
AND WIZARD
TRAINING GUIDE

SIRONA KNIGHT

CITADEL PRESS
Kensington Publishing Corp.
www.kensingtonbooks.com

To the wizards in my life, my husband Michael and my son Sky, to author J. K. Rowling for writing the Harry Potter books, and to all of you who love the magic in them.

Thank you for reading this book and making the magic real!

CITADEL PRESS books are published by

Kensington Publishing Corp.
850 Third Avenue
New York, NY 10022

"Can You Imagine?" by Robert F. Potts, is reprinted courtesy of the author.

All Kensington titles, imprints, and distributed lines are available at special quantity discounts for bulk purchases for sales promotions, premiums, fund raising, educational, or institutional use. Special book excerpts or customized printings can also be created to fit specific needs. For details, write or phone the office of the Kensington special sales manager: Kensington Publishing Corp., 850 Third Avenue, New York, NY 10022, attn: Special Sales Department, phone 1-800-221-2647.

Citadel Press and the Citadel logo are trademarks of Kensington Publishing Corp.

First printing June 2001

10 9 8 7 6 5 4 3 2 1

Printed in the United States of America

Cataloging data may be obtained from the Library of Congress.

ISBN 0-8065-2213-5

CONTENTS

Acknowledgments   vi

1. Witches and Wizards   1
2. Your Magical Altar and Tools   14
3. Magical Timing   39
4. Magic Potions   52
5. Magic Rituals and Spells   90
6. Divination   127
7. Animal Magic and Shapeshifting   152
8. Defense Against the Dark Arts   167
9. Continuing Your Witch and Wizard Training   180

Bibliography   183

ACKNOWLEDGMENTS

I WOULD LIKE TO ESPECIALLY thank and acknowledge Bruce Bender for his continued faith in my writing. Blessings and loving thanks to my agent, Lisa Hagan at Paraview, for her support, integrity, and friendship. I would like to respectfully acknowledge and thank Margaret Wolf for her patience and persistence and many thanks and heartfelt appreciation to Renata Butera for her enthusiasm and keen editing. I would also like to gratefully thank Steven Zacharius, my publisher, for bringing magic into the world by publishing books like this one.

Loving thanks to my family and friends, especially my mother, Betty, my sister, Katy, and my niece, Stephanie (I might add, all of whom have read every one of the Harry Potter books). Much love and heartfelt thanks to my teachers and to the witches and wizards of the College of the Sun in Chico, California; and respectful and loving thanks to the many light-filled goddesses and gods, to my ancestors, and the sacred land.

A special thank you to everyone at *Magical Blend Magazine*, especially Michael Langevin, the editor and publisher, for his continued support, friendship, and enthusiasm. And heartfelt thanks and many blessings to Melissa Dragich, Heidi Ellen Robinson, and Donovan for their continued kindness and friendship.

I would also like to thank and acknowledge the witches and wizards in my life, including Patricia Telesco, Dorothy Morrison, Skye Alexander, A. J. Drew, Raven Grimassi, Phyllis Currot, Raymond Buckland, Gerina Dunwich, Lady Sabrina, Z. Budapest, Starhawk, Marion Weinstein, Silver RavenWolf, R. J. Stewart, and Josephine Stewart. Thank you all for sharing your magic with me and helping the circle grow ever stronger.

May joy and magic be yours, forever and a day!

1

WITCHES
AND WIZARDS

Can you imagine a world without witches,
A world with all people the same?
Where the only known dragons are hiding in books,
And children are terribly tame?
A world without magic would be sad indeed.
I cannot imagine the pain
Of having a world where there's no Santa Claus,
Where wizards are searched for in vain.
Can you imagine a world without spells,
That science and businesses run?
And think of the sadness a unicorn feels
When he no longer plays in the sun.
Can you imagine a world without witches,
No elves, and no magical pools?
And can you imagine how dull it would be
If all that we had were the schools?
I cannot imagine a world without witches,
A world with no magical wand.
A world without beauty, or even a dream,
Or a wood sprite of whom to be fond.
They say I should grow up and be more mature,
Like a normal adult ought to do.
But I'd rather, at night, go to dance with a witch,
And I'll bet that you feel that way, too.

—Robert F. Potts, "Can You Imagine?"

Belief in witches and wizards is worldwide. From the earliest times, stories of magic such as the story of Merlin in King Arthur's court, have continued to capture the interest and imagination of each new generation of readers. Now with the unparalleled popularity of the Harry Potter books by J. K. Rowling, a whole new generation—both young and old—are adventuring into the magical world of witches and wizards.

Wise women, medicine men, High Priestesses and Priests, and gods and goddesses were some of the first witches and wizards. For example, Merlin the Magician was originally the Celtic god Myrddyn (pronounced Mirthin). Through time, Myrddyn transformed into the Merlin we are familiar with in the story of Camelot.

Traditionally, folklore, mythology, and legends portray witches and wizards as knowing how to shape shift and fly through the air. They have remarkable powers of divination, can become invisible at will, and have supernatural strength and Divine protection. They can move inanimate objects and create magical patterns to get what they want. Witches and wizards also know how to make magic potions and do magic rituals, spells, and charms to produce desired effects.

In terms of this guide, witches and wizards are people trained in the ways of magic—including but not only divination, spellcasting, potions, shapeshifting, and defense against the Dark Arts. Up until now, there have been very few guides available for learning about how to become a witch or wizard. This guide shows you how to do just that, providing hands-on magical training for the uninitiated.

As you read through the pages of this book and go through the training methods, you will enter a world that up until now may have seemed like only a fantasy. The non-magical would like you to believe that magic doesn't exist, but every Christmas their efforts get thwarted. Like the Grinch who continually tries to stamp out anything positive and happy, the non-magicals try to ignore the existence of magic because they are afraid of and hate anything strange or mysterious.

Because of this attitude, witches and wizards have historically remained separate from the non-magical world and kept their practices secret. As more people become trained as witches and wizards and get in touch with their inner magician, this attitude is rapidly changing. And with more people believing in magic, the world, as a whole, is becoming more magical.

Witches and wizards live in both the magical and non-magical worlds. They maintain their outward appearances of civility, while at the same time harboring the last vestiges of a tradition that is as old as the proverbial hills. In fact, in Ireland, these hills are the sacred and magical home of the faeries, known as the sihde (pronounced shee).

Transforming what seems like fiction into nonfiction can look like a difficult task, but it isn't. After all, most fiction is based on life—on nonfiction, and truth is often stranger than fiction. Such is the case with witchcraft. So keep an open mind and get ready to attain your goals and make your life magical!

ENTERING THE MAGICAL WORLD

Magic, in the form of the Mystery Traditions, has been passed down since the dawn of humanity. It has become interwoven into modern culture to the extent that when anything out of the ordinary happens, it is called "magical" or "miraculous." So many magical things happen that we can't explain in terms of scientific black-and-white reality. Some days you get up and everything seems to work out for you. Have you ever wondered why? On these days, you get a feeling that you can do no wrong and that everything will go smoothly. This is what magic is all about, making each moment work for you on a level you've only fantasized about up until now.

The people who make extraordinary things happen every day of their life are called witches and wizards. More than "hocus, pocus, dominocus," magic requires effort and diligence on the part of the witch and wizard. Every time you do a technique, spell, or ritual, you are setting up a magical pattern. This pattern is like a seed that you nurture and care for until it comes to fruition.

Magic is a formula for getting what you want out of life. By believing in the possibilities of magic, you open your mind up to a world where anything is possible. On one hand, this can be scary because of its unlimited implications and responsibilities. On the other hand, by creating magical patterns to attain your goals, you can manifest your deepest desires and make your dreams come true.

As children, we all believed in the possibilities of magic. As we grew older, we were told to grow up and accept life for what it is, no matter how mundane or dull this prospect might be. Like Peter Pan, author J. K. Rowling's Harry Potter stories bring magic back to the forefront of everyday life, bridging the gap between children and adults as the stories appeal to both. My nine-year-old niece just read *Harry Potter and the Goblet of Fire*. When we were sitting down to a family dinner, my sister remarked to me, "Anyone who writes a 734-page story that is so interesting that kids willingly read it deserves my unending thanks as a parent."

This points to the fact that even though as adults, we suppress our belief in the magical aspects of life, we never truly stop believing. When stories like the Harry Potter books find their way into print, the ravenous reading public devours them. The magic is still within us, just waiting to be activated. It is so powerful, so innate, that it can't be ignored.

As if programmed into our DNA, magic is a repetitive theme in both art and spirituality. In art, it is creative inspiration, and in spirituality, a miracle. Either way, an event is magical when it doesn't fit with normal expectations. By labeling these kind of events as either creative or miraculous, we avoid having to deal with their magical implications. This of course becomes a classic case of avoidance. What are we avoiding? In this case, it is the idea of losing control, of having magical occurrences or miracles in our life. We pray for magic to happen, and then when it does, it frightens us.

Magic is all around us whether you choose to acknowledge it or not. Science, for having all the answers, still falls short in their explanations. Ultimately, science and spirituality must come into a balance, where both concepts are integrated into one. This union, this Oneness, is the wellspring of all magic. It is the accumulative power of all that is, was, will ever be, and more.

By becoming a witch or wizard you begin to unleash the magical power in your life. Nowhere is it written that life is supposed to be regimented into mundane routines that only serve to opiate the masses. Although it's true that routine is a necessary practicality, it's the unexpected that really makes life interesting and stirs things up!

To become a witch or wizard means you have mastered the blending of science and spirituality. The word "magic" actually stems from "Magi," the name for Persian priests who were the first astronomers and healers. In terms of this book, what you will learn is the ancient art and craft that is actually the science of magic (Yes! There is a science to magic). Like Merlin, and a host of others both fictional and historical, you will learn how to wield the tools of the craft, make magic potions, and cast magic spells. I guarantee your life will never be mundane again. It will be filled to the brim with magic!

FAMOUS WITCHES AND WIZARDS

Combating the darkness that pervades our world is usually the thing that makes good witches and wizards famous. An illustrious group who have done just that includes Merlin, Alberich, Morgana, Nostradamus, Circe, Lugh, Cliodna, and Odin, to name just a few. Each have attributes and skills that they use in ways that move beyond ordinary reality. Each famous witch and wizard has a magical talent that makes them famous. The following describes some of the more famous witches and wizards, some of whom are legends and others are from fiction.

Within the land of the dwarves, whose magical skills include the making of Odin's magic ring and Freya's magic necklace, Alberich is the king. He lives in a magnificent subterranean palace studded with precious gems. In the *Nibelungenlied*, Alberich is the guardian of the Nibelung hoard (they protect a cursed treasure). He gives the Icelandic hero, Siegfried, a cloak of invisibility and a sword called Balmung. Dwarves are expert craftsmen, and the dwarf energy is excellent when doing magical works that are tied to the element of Earth, such as rocks made into jewelry, talismans, and amulets.

The Greek Goddess Circe controls the destiny of life, and as such is called the She-Falcon as well as the deathbird. As the dark moon goddess, she is the one who spins the fate of all living things. Ancient Greek writers called her "Circe of the Braided Tresses" because she could manipulate the forces of creation and destruction by knots and braids in her hair, from which Homer calls her "the fair-haired goddess." In Homer's *Odyssey*, Circe turns Ulysses' crew into animals and then later helps Ulysses by telling him what to say to Tiresias in Hades, and forecasts the dangers he will face on his journey. Circe and the Witch of Endor both hold the distinction of being the most famous witches in folklore.

A fairy queen of Munster, a provence in Southern Ireland, associated with May Day celebrations, Cliodna (pronounced Cleena), is said to be the daughter of Geban, the last druid in Ireland. She is an Irish goddess of beauty, the sea, and afterlife, and the daughter of the Celtic sea god Manannan. As such, she rules the Land of Promise, an otherworld where there is no violence or death. When she assumes human form, Cliodna is the most beautiful woman on earth. Songbirds and sea birds are her sacred animals and nine is her number. She has three magical birds that heal the sick by singing them to sleep. She is also the matron of waves, in particular the ninth wave of every series of waves breaking on the shore. A beach is the best place to call upon her, since she may take the form of a sea bird or a large wave.

Albus Dumbledore is the headmaster at Hogwarts School of Witchcraft and Wizardry in J. K. Rowling's Harry Potter books. He is best known for his defeat of the dark wizard Grindlewald. He also discovered the twelve uses of dragon's blood and is a noted alchemist. Many say he is one of the most powerful wizards of modern times, and the only one the dark wizard Voldemort truly fears.

After being tormented by her evil stepmother and stepsisters, Cinderella received aid from her Fairy Godmother, who through the use of magic, eventually transforms Cinderella's life into a dream come true. Her Fairy Godmother's main magical talent is her ability to shape shift or transfigure objects from one shape to another, such as changing the pumpkin into a coach and Cinderella's tattered clothes into a magnificent costume fit for a princess.

Enlisting the aid of Galadriel, the Queen of the elves, Aragorn, a human king, plus a host of hobbits by the names of Bilbo, Frodo, and Sam, among others, the wizard Gandalf sets out on a quest to destroy a magic ring before it falls into the hands of the dark wizard, Sauron. In J. R. R. Tolkien's trilogy, *The Hobbit*, Gandalf is very adept at magical practices including shapeshifting, divination, and magic spells. Gandalf is considered one of the greatest of modern wizards.

Glenda the Good Witch is the one who helps Dorothy find and follow the yellow brick road, and it is only with Glenda's aid that Dorothy is able to eventually defeat the wicked witch. Glenda's magical strengths are her extraordinary use of the magical wand and her knowledge and defense against the Dark Arts. For example, she can appear and disappear with the wave of her wand.

The Irish God, Lugh, is master of all the magical arts. His magical tools include a spear that moves and fights on its own. As a member of Divine family of the Tuatha De Danann, Lugh is part of the wizards and witches who conquer Ireland, and later move into the hills and mounds of Ireland, transforming into the magical faeries that reside in the land. His power now sleeps in the land. If you know how, you can awaken and utilize this energy to attain your magical goals.

More stories exist about the magical exploits of Merlin than any other wizard. As a close adviser and mentor to King Arthur and the Knights of the Round Table, Merlin is renowned for his skills in shapeshifting, potions, and magic spells. In one such spell, Merlin is reputed to have magically transported the huge megaliths of Stonehenge from Ireland to their present location on the Salisbury Plains, a distance of over three hundred miles.

Morgana's exploits are known in many cultures and as such she has acquired various names including Morrigan and Morrigu. She is the "great queen" of Irish mythology who aids the hero Cuchulain in his battles to right the wrongs of the world. Her main magical ability is her knowledge of the Dark Arts and her ability to defend herself against any kind of black magic. To have her on your side is highly advantageous, but to incur her wrath is foolish.

One of the great wizards of divination, Nostradamus, made prophecies that are still accurate after six hundred years. An early student of the magical arts, Nostradamus learned to expertly read magical patterns like no other wizard. His prophetic quatrains are still avidly read and interpreted for revelations about the future of this world.

Like the god Math in the Celtic tradition, the Norse god Odin hears all things through the use of his two ravens. His birds are basically extensions of himself. In his thirst for knowledge, Odin discovers the secret of the runes, which become one of his tools for divination. Odin, with the aid of Thor and the other Norse gods, battle the giants who are the source of all chaos. When Odin and his brothers defeat the giant Ymir, they use his body to fashion life as we know it, including the Earth, the sky, and other realms of reality. His main strength stems from his great wisdom and knowledge of magic.

In the Old Testament, the Witch of Endor honors the request of Saul, first king of Israel, when she conjures up Samuel's spirit. Samuel tells Saul that he and his two sons will die in battle the next day. This prophecy was done at a time when the ways of magic were being outlawed by the non-magical, who were increasingly gaining influence. The Witch of Endor's main magical strength is her ability to channel spirit energies, from which she gains knowledge and insight. It was her magical talent that drew Saul to her in the first place.

The great and powerful Wizard of Oz lives in the Emerald City, and with the aid of Dorothy, the Scarecrow, the Tin Man, and the Cowardly Lion, defeats the wicked witches of the East and West. The Wizard of Oz's greatness derives from his ability to magically empower others to excel beyond their expectations. He is purported by some to be one of the great teachers of witches and wizards.

As teacher of Obi Won Kenobi and Luke Skywalker, the wizard Yoda is a master of the forces of magic. His main skill is the ability to move objects through space, the proverbial mind over matter. With the aid of others, he is able to defeat Darth Vader and the Emperor and thwart their plan to enslave the universe. Although set in the future, Yoda is a modern wizard in the traditional sense because he moves the force in strange and mysterious ways. The way of the Jedi is the way of wizards. They are one and the same. The "force" is "Oneness," the infinite energy of all that is. It is this Oneness that you tap into for successful magic making.

WHITE AND BLACK MAGIC

Magic is either positive or negative, depending on the intention of the magician. Positive, white magic, brings beneficial things into your life. For example, making a talisman can bring you good luck. Negative, black magic, is used to harm people and cause negative events. Black witches and wizards use energies associated with the dark side. These negative energies aid dark, evil wizards and witches in their black magic, harmful works that are intended to bring bad luck and cause harm to the recipient.

Each of you as you enter the witch and wizard training, are given the age-old choice; to go with the light or to go with the dark side. The choice is ultimately yours, but be warned, if you chose the dark side, it will eventually destroy you.

Choosing the dark side is similar to joining the mafia. Once you're in, you're a member for life. The initial appeal of the Dark Arts is the immediate sensation of power, but in the long term, negativity eats at you much like it ate at Darth Vader in "Star Wars," until he became so disfigured that he became a monster and no longer resembled a human being.

Those who subscribe to dark ways gave in to a dark polarity that at one time or another rears its ugly head in all of us. Those who adhere to positive magic represent the bright polarity, the polarity that balances the darkness and brings order to the chaos.

The light always overcomes the dark. The dawn always rises. If the darkness was more powerful and had the upper hand, then Adolph Hitler would have, without question, won World War II. But he didn't. Those who practice the Dark Arts will find themselves on the losing end of things. A dark wizard's lack of success is due to negative energy's preponderance to feed upon itself.

In the short run, practicing the Dark Arts will make you mean and vindictive because you have to build up a certain amount of negative energy to do black magic. This brings you some instant gratification, but in the long run you end up like Faust and darkness comes looking for your soul, at which point, you have no way out. When you turn to the darkness, you cannot turn back.

UNDERSTANDING THE NON-MAGICALS

Non-magicals are people who fear anything out of the ordinary, and hate anything they can't control. At the first sight of anything strange or mysterious, they turn a blind eye and convince themselves that it just doesn't exist.

The non-magicals strive to be well-respected. They order their world into neat boxes and compartments, systematically excluding anything out of the ordinary. In this way, they can ignore everything that doesn't fit within their rigid standards. Their reality is always the only reality, and everyone else is, of course, nuts. They are slow to realize what is right, but quick to criticize what they feel is wrong. Working off the negative makes them crotchety, especially in their old age. There are only so many times you can tolerate listening to a non-magical whine about what is wrong with the world, with no attempt to correct it.

The non-magicals are the Grinches, always trying to throw a wrench in everything, from Christmas to new ideas and experiences. Standing on the street corner, they tell all the kids that Santa Claus isn't real, that he doesn't exist, and that everything good happened in the past. They use their non-magical attitudes as a security blanket, a blanket which can be comforting, but in the end is suffocating. The truth of the matter is that each and every one of us is a witch or wizard, but the non-magicals are those people who choose to ignore their Divine magical abilities.

You must remain open to the unexpected for magic to happen in your life. Predictability breeds a sameness that excludes anything strange or mysterious. These unusual events are the ones that propel life forward and make it special. When life becomes magical, greatness happens.

If non-magicals tell you that you shouldn't be practicing magic, or that you are on the wrong path, use that as a sign telling you that you are exactly where you should be. As a rule, the non-magical perception is just the opposite of what it should be. So when uncle Ernie tells you that you ought to be selling drill bits, you can laugh him off, and then cast a spell to move toward what it is you really do want to do. You are the one that has to live with your choices, not Uncle Ernie, regardless of his "good" intentions. Magic is all about making choices. Once you've made the choice, do everything you can to make it work for you.

HOW THE WITCH AND WIZARD TRAINING WORKS

The chapters of this book are divided into different magical subjects such as potions, spell casting, divination, shapeshifting and animal magic, and defense against the Dark Arts. Within each chapter, there is an overview of the subject, plus step-by-step instructions on how to do the works. Blending traditional witch and wizard training with recent New Age discoveries gives this guide depth and breadth in its approach to teaching magic.

As you make the potions and cast the spells in this book, be sure to use Divine energies with whom you are in tune. These energies can come in any form: goddess, god, Oneness, pure light, spirit animals, angels, and so forth. Use positive energies that are in alignment with who you are. This can be done easily by sitting down alone and getting in touch with the energies that exist all around you.

We all have Divine energies in the form of guardian angels, spirit animals, gods, and goddesses, that help us. Often these energies take the form of our ancestors. These powerful energies can be invoked anytime you want to make magic. When you do this, it separates you from the non-magicals. It's often hard to deny what is inside of you as it propels you forward with little more than your tacit consent. There is a force that drives us that is both within our physical being as well as within the magical ethers that make up the energetic layers of our being. Learning to integrate the two is what magic and this book is all about.

In the past five centuries, we humans have become scientific and technical in our approach to life. In the next millennium, we will be required to integrate this scientific data into the spiritual side of life. We are but stagnate black and white shadows without magic. It is the color that brightens our life experiences. By applying a little magic, we are no longer just shadowy stick figures, but instead we become colorful and well-rounded individuals. This book offers ways for you to color your world using the magic techniques within its pages. It provides the paint and paint brushes. You provide the canvas. You will learn that there is a world filled with magic where you fit in perfectly. Remember, magic is real. Things do go bump in the night, and they will continue to do so as long as there is life on this planet. With a little magical training, at least you can learn to identify what it is that's doing the bumping.

WHAT'S EXPECTED OF YOU
IN YOUR STUDIES

For starters, the first thing that is expected of you is for you to go out and bring light into the world. Second, you need to apply yourself and become the best witch or wizard that you can be. Intend and expect to make miracles and magic happen every day by applying the methods in this book. As with learning anything, the more you practice and apply yourself, the further you will get in the training.

Witch and wizard training is timeless, and has proven effective for many aspiring students down through the ages. I'm sure these tried-and-true methods will work for you, too. Knowledge is most important when it stirs us to move to the next level of development. With practice, we are all capable of achieving this goal. Baseball players don't usually hit home runs the first time at bat, and people don't become witches and wizards until they practice and become proficient in the magical arts. By being well-versed in the information contained in this guide, you will be well on your way to becoming a witch or wizard in your own right.

You carry the flame, the light of life. How you illuminate your world is a matter of how you apply your light. When you become magically adept, you can light the night sky like a brilliant star, ridding the world of ignorance and fear, and its progeny, darkness. You are born a child of the light, seeking to return home. Like a candle in the wind, you flicker and flame into the dawn, where you are once again, reborn into the light.

As a witch and wizard, you light the fires of Oneness. You brighten the world like the sun does every day. You learn to brighten your corner of the universe, and through your light, the dark land becomes a little lighter. Dark and light have battled through time eternal, and we are merely the latest heroes, heroines, and victims. We battle the bad guys, the dark wizards, so that life remains a bright bastion of hope, forever alive and forever magical.

2

Your Magical Altar and Tools

ASPIRING WITCHES AND WIZARDS gather their magical supplies before they start to do magic. They collect spellbooks, cauldrons, broomsticks, robes, and wands. Wands have the power to open doorways into other magical dimensions. Wands draw energy from these other worlds that affect what is going on in this world. When doing magic, the primary connection is between this world and the world of the Divine. For purposes of this book I call the Divine by the name Oneness, a concept that is inclusive of all philosophies. Oneness is all things manifested and unmanifested.

When doing magic, it is customary to place your wand and other magical tools on your altar. This is the sacred table of the Goddess. The word altar means "high place," which is symbolic not so much of altitude, but of attitude. It is a connecting place to Oneness, where the sacred and mundane meet as well as a magical working surface that holds your tools, focals, and other items. Standing before your altar, you make potions, spin spells, do rituals, and ask for divine guidance. Approaching the altar with its tools, lit candles, and burning incense, immediately creates an aura of mystery and magic.

When building an altar, use a sturdy surface such as a table, trunk, bookshelf, or fireplace mantle. Garden benches, patio tables, large flat-topped stones, or tree stumps work well as outdoor altars.

Set your altar up in the north quarter or corner of your magical space. North is the direction of Divine knowledge and ancestral wisdom. Spread an altar cloth out on the altar surface to protect it from dripping wax, and arrange your magical tools and focals. The altar cloth can be made of any fabric, although natural fabrics, such as linen, cotton, silk, and wool, are more durable. Traditionally red, your altar cloth can be any color. I suggest you change it regularly to match the seasons. You can also decorate your cloth with embroidery or paint magic symbols on it like pentacles, stars, spirals, moons, and runes.

The left side of the altar is the creative, nurturing side, dedicated to the Goddess, while the right side is the power side of the altar dedicated to the God. Place your tools on the altar accordingly. For example, the athame is a male, fire tool that goes on the right side, while the bowl is a female, earth tool that goes on the left side. If you like, you can place an image of the Goddess (on the left) and God (on the right) on your altar. Make your gestures and cast your spells before them.

I like to change my altar with the changing seasons and holidays. For example, in the spring I put fresh flowers like daffodils and tulips on the altar. In the winter, I decorate the surface with evergreen boughs and pine cones.

THE THREE STEPS OF MAGIC

Your altar provides the sacred space for doing magic to attain your goals. The three basic steps of magic are: 1. intention and expectation; 2. desire; and 3. merging. Together, they are a basic formula for patterning energy. Another way to see the steps is: 1. conceiving, 2. creating, and 3. experiencing.

You can apply the three steps to all your magic making. First, you need really understand what your intentions are and what it is you expect, and most of all, that you really want it. Second, you must have a strong desire to attain your magical goal. Third, you must merge with Oneness, with divinity, as deeply as possible, and then a little deeper still, allowing your intention, expectation, and desire to flow out of you and move out into the world. Imagine releasing thought energy so strong that it becomes real!

MERGING

Merging connects you with Oneness and is the key to magical patterns and spellwork. It is the natural feeling you get when you are in love, walking in an old-growth forest, or watching the sun set over the ocean. Merging is the feeling you get when you are in tune with everything and at one with it all. It becomes your doorway to magic. The deeper you merge, the more powerful your magic.

When you merge with Oneness, you may experience sensations of relaxation, peacefulness, well-being, spinning, flying, whirling, and lightheadedness or heaviness. You may feel like you are floating as you feel yourself being both everything and nothing, all at the same time.

You can enhance your merging experience by using breathing exercises, staring at candlelight, dancing, chanting, as well as listening to special music, drumming, and using visualization techniques. The goal in merging is to become one with everything, to just diffuse like a cloud into the universe.

Merging is also a way to move beyond time and space. By merging deeply enough, you can view the past in such a way that you are actually seen in the past as an apparition. Deep merges can provide vivid details about places, people, and events. When your merging experience is less deep, the images are less definite and more fleeting.

MAGIC FOCALS

Focals are used for amplifying, focusing, and concentrating magical energy. They should blend with the potion you are making or spell you are casting. I like to use many focals blended together. You will find that focals like food, music, scented oils, candles, incense, and decorations, all add more power to your magic. The following is a list of focals used in magic.

Visual Focals—Sight. Things you look at. Examples include photographs, symbols, drawings, paintings, statues, flowers.

Auditory Focals—Sound. Things you hear. Examples are music, singing, chanting, drumming, humming, breathing, ocean, fountains, birds.

Gustatory Focals—Taste. Things you taste. Examples are food, beverages, and the salt on your skin.

Kinesthetic Focals—Touch. Things you can touch. Examples are skin, plants, fabrics such as velvet, carved chalices, shells, and crystals.

Olfactory Focals—Smell. Things you can smell. Examples are scented oils, scented candles, foods, and incense.

Intuitive Focals—Psychic Sense. Things you can sense intuitively. Examples are ritual jewelry and talismans.

WITCH AND WIZARD MAGIC TOOLS

Magic tools are filled with Divine energies, and in the process they become energetically alive. The tools that you gather together, consecrate, and use regularly in ritual and magic are more than symbols that trigger your subconscious—they are essentially a part of you. They are imprinted with your energy signature. The following is a list of the tools that witches and wizards use on a regular basis.

ATHAME

A double-edge knife or dagger that you purchase new. The athame is a symbol of creative fire, and is used as a pointer to define space, such as cutting a magic circle. Your athame can also be used to cut magical foods, to inscribe candles, and to carve runes. The athame's edges are dulled for magical use to avoid accidents. (Remember to keep all knives in a safe place and away from children.)

BELL

A feminine symbol of the Goddess, the bell is usually rung at the beginning and ending of a ritual or spell. It can be used to summon Divine energies, as a fertility charm, and for protection against negativity.

BOLLINE

A knife with a white handle that is used to harvest herbs, slice foods, and inscribe candles. Not normally used for spells and rituals.

BOOK OF SHADOWS OR MAGIC JOURNAL

A private journal of your magical experiences. Rituals, potions, spells, thoughts, and ideas are written in it.

BOWL

The bowl represents the powers of earth and North point. The universal purifier salt, dry or mixed with water, goes into the bowl. You can also use clean soil instead of salt.

BROOM OR BESOM

Dating back as far as ancient Egypt, the besom (pronounced beh-sum) was once a wooden staff with a fan of feathers. Used for protection and purification purposes, a magic broom is made of straw or grass tied around a leafy branch of pine, oak, fir, lavender, or rosemary. It is used to clean your ritual circle of unwanted energies. Called the "Faery's Horse," your magic broom can be used for astral traveling. Different kinds of brooms are used for different things. For example, hawthorn besoms are best for handfastings. Both people jump over the broomstick to show they are joined as one and to seal their union. Oak besoms can be used as powerful tools for personal protection and to draw in ancestral energies and knowledge.

Making Your Own Magic Broom

You can make your own magic broom. Your besom won't physically fly through the air, but it can be used for protection, sweeping negativity away, and astral projection. A state-of-the-art witch's and wizard's besom sports a superfine handle of ash, treated with consecrated ritual oil, with the broom's name hand-carved on it. Each individually selected broomstraw is chosen for its strength and beauty. Follow these nine easy steps to make your own magic broom.

1. Begin by selecting the wood for your broom. Traditional choices include ash, birch, willow, oak, and pine.
2. Next, saw a branch to just the length you need (the length is dependent upon your height). Do this carefully so you don't damage the tree. Remember to thank the tree spirit for the branch.
3. Use your athame or bolline to carve your broom's name on it with runes, symbols, or letters.
4. Rub scented oil that's been consecrated, on the broom staff to seal it.
5. You can make the broomstraws out of straw, wheat, lavender, or heather, to name a few. They need to be about half the length of the broom staff. Carefully select the broomstraws for their strength. When cutting the straws, add about two inches. If you use straw, soak the straws in water to make them more flexible.
6. Assemble the broomstraws around the branch, making the stalk tips even. Also, make sure the straw is equally distributed around the broom staff.
7. With the added two inches of straw, bind the broomstraw to the staff with flexible willow branches or strong twine.

8. You can decorate your broom by adding things to it such as feathers, beads, acorns, or small pine cones.

9. When you want to use your besom, stand in the center of your magic circle and move clockwise (sunwise), using your broom to sweep from the center outward. With each sweeping motion, imagine the area being washed energetically with a cobalt blue light, while saying something like:

> *Sweep out evil, sweep out ill,*
> *Where I do the Lady's will.*
> *Besom, besom, Lady's broom*
> *Sweep out darkness, sweep out doom.*
> *So be it! Blessed be!*

CANDLES

Almost always used in magic making, candles are associated with the fire element. They speak a magical language, the words being expressed by the flickering and dancing of the candle flame, the billowing of the smoke, and the popping of the hot wax. Candle chatter, and the direction of the flame, denote magical communication. First choose the candle color that matches your magical goal. Then dress and empower the candle by anointing the candle body with scented oil, starting at the center of the candle and rubbing the oil all over both ends. As you do this, focus on attaining your magical goal. Be sure to match the oil scent with your goal.

COLOR CORRESPONDENCES

Color influences everything you see and can be used to power your magic making. Use the following table as a template for integrating color into your magical spells and rituals.

Color	Magical Uses
White	Universal candle color that can be used for all works. Inspiration, divine guidance, power, purity, love, motivation, peace, protection, Oneness
Gray	Mastery, balance, wisdom, merging, invention, discovery, protection
Black	Banishing negative energies, ending relationships, transforming negative energy to positive energy, the shadow self, dream magic
Blue	Tranquility, purification, healing, divination, travel, loyalty, psychic protection, perception, harmony, peace, moving energy, higher wisdom
Purple	Psychic awareness, ancestral lore, respect, sacredness, consecration, offensive protection, dream magic, wisdom, spiritual healing, power, leadership
Pink	Friendship, romance, love, calming emotions, loving and accepting children, kinship, kindness, compassion
Rose	Ecstasy, Divine love, enlightenment, romance
Red	Strength, survival, action, passion, lust, sexuality, vitality, virility, courage, blood, rebirth, focus, power, animation, intense desire
Orange	Business, joy, generosity, success, gladness, mirth, ease and comfort, prosperity, plenty, the home, friendship, happiness, meditation, fair play, justice, productive action
Yellow	Attraction, persuasion, imagination, knowledge, learning, teaching, mental agility, understanding, cognition, truth, comprehension, communication, perception
Green	Fertility, creativity, birth, healing, ambition, prosperity, abundance, money, regeneration, renewal, growth, nature, good luck

Brown   Grounding, stability, pets, animals, potential, nurturing, birth and rebirth, family, home, common sense

Gold   Wealth, increase, attraction, expanded awareness, creativity, strength, security, solar energy

Silver   Peace, dream magic, lunar and stellar power, ancestral communication, divine insight, clairvoyance, astral travel, divination

CAULDRON

Your cauldron is a powerful ritual tool that represents the powers of water and the womb of the Goddess. A cauldron is a three-legged pot with its opening smaller than its base used for brewing potions and holding herbs. Candles can be set inside it and allowed to safely burn out. Cauldrons can also be used for scrying when filled with water or oil.

CHALICE

Symbol of water and the West (or all directions), the chalice holds water or wine. It is a sacred vessel made of stone, clay, lead-free pewter, silver, or glass, representing the Goddess.

CLOAK OR ROBE

Robes and cloaks are part of the attire of witches and wizards, particularly when doing magic potions, rituals, spells, and all the things that witches and wizards do. Although your cloak or robe may not make you invisible, it acts like a magical skin. It can be made of any fabric, any color, any design. The reason it is reserved for magic is because whenever you put on your cloak or robe, you automatically move into a magical frame of mind. Men sometimes wear kilts, instead of robes. Contemporary groups often dispense with robes, wearing only street clothes.

MAKING YOUR MAGIC CLOAK

The easiest cloak to make is by cutting out a large square or rectangular piece of fabric. Hem it all the way around. The cloak can be draped, and then pinned at the shoulders with a large broach. Your cloak can also double as a meditation blanket. The beauty of this type of cloak is it can be recycled into something else when you find a fitted cloak that you like better.

You can also make a poncho-like cloak by cutting a large circle of fabric out from the middle of your originally square or rectangle cloth and then cutting a neck hole in it where your head goes. This is a good choice for children because it's easy to make and there are no fastenings. For adults, you will need to piece fabric yardage together to get a diameter that is twice the length you want. If you cut the neck hole off center, your cloak will have a defined front and back to it.

The half-circle cloak is another option. Made from a half-circle of fabric, with the diameter twice the desired length, it hangs off your shoulders. Use frog fasteners, a buckle, or a large broach to fasten your cloak. Ribbon ties don't work because they have a tendency to choke you when the cloak slips back.

CORD

Symbolic of the cord of life, your cord should measure nine feet long with a knot at one end to anchor it to a stick, and knots at 4 ½ feet, 6 ½ feet, and 7 ½ feet. It is used to draw a magic circle, a pentacle, or you can wrap it around the waist of your robe or cloak.

CRYSTALS AND GEMSTONES

Fondly called the stars within the Earth, quartz crystals are used in magic because they act as natural energy magnifiers. Both quartz

crystal and the human body contain silicon, which forms the physical basis for our connection with quartz. Crystals and gemstones are
powerful tools that can be used for healing, protection, and mental
clarity. Please refer to my book, *The Pocket Guide to Crystals and Gemstones* (Crossing Press, 1998), for more information about how to use
stones for magical purposes. The following table lists stones and their
magical uses.

Stone	*Magical Uses*
Amethyst	Protection, healing, love, divination, astral travel, banishing nightmares, mental clarity
Carnelian	Personal power, sexuality, creativity, past lives, protection, courage, focus, motivation
Citrine	Mental quickness, dream magic, dispels negativity, insight, empowerment, shapeshifting
Clear Quartz	The master stone for all magic, healing, divination, meditation, shapeshifting, astral travel, insight, higher consciousness, purification, protection, balancing energy
Diamond	Strength, healing, empowerment, inspiration, protection, memory, prosperity, endurance, clarity
Emerald	Sexuality, love, balancing emotions, patience, growth, healing, meditation
Garnet	Friendship, faithfulness, strength, protection, virility, trust, balance
Jade	Love, protection, wealth, purification, meditation, harmony, dispelling negativity
Lapis Lazuli	Psychic development, divination, shapeshifting, empowerment, moving energy, knowledge, wealth, astral travel, creativity, protection

Malachite	Shapeshifting, willpower, communication with nature, peaceful sleep, visions, healing, prosperity
Moonstone	Moon magic, good fortune, fertility, love, lunar healing, receptivity, intuition, divination, artistic pursuits, balancing emotions
Pyrite	Wealth, prosperity, plenty (To ensure prosperity, your piece of pyrite should hold together and not flake apart.)
Rose Quartz	Friendship, love, romance, balances emotions, divine inspiration, adapting to change, forgiveness, attunement, faith, fertility, compassion, opens the heart, represents feminine energy
Ruby	Strength, magical power, protection, insight, creativity, passion, friendship, clarity, astral travel, activates the life force, attracts wealth
Turquoise	Astral travel, dream magic, communication with your ancestors, elemental wisdom, motivation, healing, faery magic, attunement

Drum

A bridge to the spirit or Otherworld, the drum is associated with the Air and Earth elements and is used for focusing, merging, communicating with the ancestral spirits, as well as enhancing creativity, astral travel, goal attainment, and divination. Drumming almost immediately puts you into an altered state of consciousness. The head of a person's drum is broken when they die as a way to free their spirit.

Incense Censor With Incense

Incense stirs the conscious mind. Associated with Fire and Air, incense is often used on the altar to attract helpful spiritual energies. To communicate with the Goddess and God, say your prayers and wishes

directly into incense smoke. You can make your own incense or purchase ready-made sticks and cones. Be sure the incense you use
matches your magical goal. You can use a purchased incense burner,
use an abalone shell, or you can put a layer of sand or pebbles inside
a bowl as a base for the charcoal block(s). Some people prefer using
thurible burners, which are three-legged dishes. Potpads, handles, or
a chain are a necessity if you are going to move the burner when it's
hot. If you are sensitive to smoke, you can substitute essential oils
and an aromatherapy diffuser, or you can put a few drops of essential
oil in a small pan of boiling water or on a lightbulb.

Scrying Mirror

Your scrying mirror is used to look into the future, create protective
devices, and help you understand your inner self. You can use a full-
length mirror with three panels, a regular mirror, a black scrying
mirror, or a large, flat piece of polished obsidian as your mirror. Cover
your mirror with a black drape when you aren't using it.

Oils and Herbs

Representing the many deities and all of the elements, both herbs
and essential oils are valued for their magical energies. Oils are used
in ritual baths, sachets, charms, incense, anointing candles, consecrating magical tools, on your altar, and anointing your body. A scent
can immediately put you in a magical state of mind. Sometimes herbs
are burned over charcoal blocks on the altar. Herbs are also used in
candle magic, sachets, magic potions, as offerings to the Goddess and
God, in ritual baths, cooking, and in scented oils.

Pentagram and Pentacle

The master symbol of a modern witch or wizard, the pentacle (a
pentagram surrounded by a circle), is today what the peace sign was
to the 1960s. Most witches and wizards wear pentacle amulets and
use them in magic making. The pentagram, a five-pointed star, is used

to symbolize the Earth and its properties. It represents all of the elemental powers and the human microcosm. The pentacle is a powerful protection device, and is also used to attract Divine energies and manifest your magical desires. You can place natural pentacles on your altar such as sand dollars and starfish. You can also make a pentacle by painting or carving flat disks of wood, stone, metal, or glass. Tile pentacles protect your altar surface from melting wax, dropping ash, and hot objects. Sometimes witches and wizards paint a very large pentacle directly on their altar surface.

STAFF

A tool of authority associated with the earth element, a staff is at least shoulder height and about 1–3 inches thick. It holds and focuses magical energy. Staffs can be roughly hewn from a tree branch or carved with intricate patterns or runes. They are best cut during a waxing moon and allowed to cure for a complete moon cycle. Sometimes viewed as a combination of the sword and wand, staffs are named for particular goddesses and gods such as Merlin's Staff. The best time to consecrate your staff is at dawn on a Sabbat such as Beltane.

SWORD

A powerful and heavy tool of command associated with the Fire element and the South, the sword can be used to focus will and magic power, for protection from harmful physical and energetic forces, and for tapping into your ancestral power and wisdom. Swords are magnificent tools for cutting your magic circle.

SYMBOLS

Magical symbols can be used to add more power and depth to your potions, spells, and rituals. They are a form of magical shorthand, and are carved on magic tools, used to consecrate sacred objects, in divination, and for personal empowerment.

TALISMAN

Symbol of the Earth, a talisman is made of metal or stone. It is charged with magical properties so that it radiates a specific field of energy. Working similar to self-charging batteries, talismans help you attain your magical goals. You can make a talisman to bring you success, uncover the truth, develop your intuition, boost your personal power, and attract love, among other things. They are carried on your person or placed on the altar during magic making to strengthen the energies you are working with.

WAND

As the witch and wizard rod of authority and power, the wand acts as an extension of the practitioner's body. Associated with the East and the Air element and made from wood, wands are shorter than staffs, usually no longer than the length of your forearm. Considered the most ancient of tools, the wand is used to direct energies; to receive and send energetic patterns from the spiritual to the material plane in such a way as to create a successful outcome in magical workings.

MAKING YOUR MAGIC WAND

You can make your wand from holly or any wood you want. They are easy and fun to construct.

Begin by timing the cutting of your wand after the moon has gone dark, on the day of a new moon, or up to three days following. Timing the cutting in this way will give the right amount of "curing" time.

Begin by finding a living tree to cut your wand from. If the tree is on someone else's property, ask permission first. Cut only as much of the branch as you need. Fruit-bearing trees such as apple work well, as do ash, oak, and madrone. You can use just about any wood for your wand, but remember, each wood has different qualities. So select a wood that matches the purpose of your wand.

Before you cut your wand, get to know the tree. Sit under the tree and notice everything about it: its bark, trunk, branches, leaves, scent, and even the sound of its voice as the wind moves through its branches.

Next, walk around the tree clockwise three times. As you do this, ask it if you can have a branch from its body. You will get some sense of yes or no. If you sense a no, find another tree, and ask again. If you get a yes, then dig a small hole in the ground at the tree's base. Pour an offering such as honey and milk into the hole, and thank the tree spirit.

Cut the branch for your wand by snapping it off the tree or carefully cutting it with sharp pruning cutters, a bolline, small ax, or similar tool. Be careful not to cut yourself. The size of your wand is based on the length of your arm. Measure from the outside bend of your elbow to the tip of your fingers.

Take your wand indoors, and use your bolline or your athame to strip off the bark and shape the wand. Do not soak the wand in water to remove the bark. Merge with the Air element when you are working on your wand to strengthen its magical power. Save all of the bark shavings, putting them on a piece of newspaper or a cloth. Then, leave the stripped wand outside or in a window in the moonlight for a full moon cycle, new to full, working on it a little each day.

During the next twenty-eight days, visit the tree you took your wand from and sprinkle the bark shavings around the base of the tree. Do this in a clockwise circle, and thank the tree again. Sing a blessing song, a favorite song, or chant to the tree as you walk around it.

Once the bark has been stripped off your wand, and the wood has dried, seal it with scented oil. Again, match the scent to the wand's magical qualities. After you oil it, use your bolline or athame to carve the wand's name on it. Then, either leave your wand natural or decorate it. For example, you can fasten a crystal in the tip, or cover the wand's body with strips of fabric, or attach feathers, shells, and small bells to it.

TREE LIST

Each tree is associated with different magical qualities. To make a powerful protection charm, take one twig each from an oak, an ash, and a thorn tree that are growing side by side. Bind the three together with a red string. As you do this say,

> *I bind together oak, ash, and thorn,*
> *May they protect me always*
> *So be it! So shall it be!*

Place the bound twigs in your bedroom, preferably under your bed. This charm will protect you from any harmful spirits in the night.

Following is a brief list of the magical qualities of several trees. Remember, before taking a part of any tree, always ask permission from the tree. This may seem odd at first. Just ask the tree silently or aloud if you can use a piece of it for a broom, wand, or staff, for example. Almost immediately, you will sense a response from the tree, either yes or no. Keep asking until you sense a response. If you don't feel any response from the tree, select another tree, and ask again. This is essential because each tree has a spirit or wight within it. Your magical tools will be strong and powerful only when you receive an affirmative response from the tree. Otherwise, you will find the tools won't respond or carry the power you intended.

Tree	Qualities
Alder	The "Battle Witch," protection, truth, purification, regeneration, resurrection, solar tree
Apple	Prophesy, love, Celtic tree of life, youth, faery tree, fertility, romance, creativity

Ash	Guardian tree, runic tree, justice, longevity
Beech	Divination, holy tree, visions, insight
Birch	Goddess tree, beginnings, new ventures, to make cradles, birth, rebirth
Blackthorn	Faery communication, divination, magic, dreams
Elder	Goddess tree, witch and wizard tree, protection, healing regeneration, used for astral travel broomsticks
Elm	Vulnerability, sensitivity, empathy, creativity
Fir	Rebirth, feminine energy, endurance, lunar tree, used to mark ley lines on the land
Hawthorn	Faery tree, divination, prophesy, wisdom
Hazel	Wisdom, insight, vision, prophesy, fertility, creativity
Laurel	Oracle tree, divining, victory, honor
Madrone	Mother tree, protection, healing, strength, love, regeneration, growth
Oak	Forest king, endurance, fertility, ancestry, love, faery tree, longevity, rebirth
Pine	Life cycles, rebirth, solar tree, inspiration
Redwood	Strength, ancestry, purification, regeneration
Rowan	Sorcerer's tree, enchantment, spellcasting, witch and faery tree
Willow	Flexibility, enchantment, dreams, water power, the stars, astral travel, inspiration
Yarrow	Divining, healing, creativity
Yew	Shelter, protection, defense

CONSECRATING YOUR MAGIC TOOLS

When you get a new tool, first smudge it thoroughly with a sage and cedar smudge stick to clear out any unwanted energies. Smudge sticks are available at health food and New Age stores as well as your local witch and wizard supply shop. Sandalwood incense smoke also works well as a cleansing agent. Another way to cleanse negative energies from your tools is to wash them with dew before sunrise just before a full moon or a Sabbat.

To consecrate your new tool, bless it with the elements of Earth (salt or soil), Air (incense), Fire (flame), Water, and Spirit (scented oil). Actually apply the element to the tool. For example, sprinkle salt on a new athame, then pass it through incense smoke, a candle flame, sprinkle it with water, and rub it with scented oil. Then hold the tool in your hands and present it to each of the four directions, moving in a clockwise circle. Next, face the altar, and say,

> *I charge this tool by the Ancient Ones,*
> *By the divine powers of the Goddess and God,*
> *By the powers of the sun, moon, planets, and stars*
> *By the powers of Earth, Air, Fire, and Water,*
> *May I attain all that I desire through this tool.*
> *Charge and bless this tool with your power Old Ones!*
> *Blessed be! As I will, so shall it be!*

You can leave your tools on your altar if you have one set up permanently, or you can put them away in a special box. I suggest you put your tools away so others don't handle and play with them. At least once a year, clean and reconsecrate each tool.

A more elaborate way to consecrate your tools and other items used in magic is by merging deeply with the divine energies of the Goddess and God, and blessing the tools with the elemental qualities they correspond to, be it Earth, Air, Fire, or Water.

- To consecrate the bowl, fill it with salt or earth, hold it upward toward the North point of your magic circle, and say,

    Generous and Divine powers of earth,
    Fill this tool with your sacred energy.
    I ask this in the name of the Goddess and God,
    Blessed be! As I will, so shall it be!

- To consecrate your incense censor, put incense in it, light it, and then hold it upward toward the East point of your magic circle, and say,

    Generous and Divine powers of air,
    Fill this tool with your sacred energy.
    I ask this in the name of the Goddess and God,
    Blessed be! As I will, so shall it be!

- To consecrate your candle holder, hold it upward toward the South point of your magic circle, and say,

    Generous and Divine powers of fire,
    Fill this tool with your sacred energy.
    I ask this in the name of the Goddess and God,
    Blessed be! As I will, so shall it be!

- To consecrate your chalice, cup, or cauldron, hold each one of them upward toward the West point of your magic circle, and say,

    Generous and Divine powers of water
    Fill this tool with your sacred energy.
    I ask this in the name of the Goddess and God,
    Blessed be! As I will, so shall it be!

To empower your tools even more, pass them through or sprinkle them with the corresponding element. For example, pass your candle holder through the flame of a candle, or sprinkle water on your chalice. When doing this, say,

> *With this element,*
> *I consecrate this tool to the Goddess and God.*
> *Blessed be! So shall it be!*

Yet another way to consecrate your magic tools is by merging and becoming one with the Divine energies, and asking them to impart their Divine energy and aspects into the tool. Actually imagine the power of the Goddess and God pouring into the object, and then use your breath to move the Divine energy into the item, by breathing in deeply and holding your breath for a few seconds while you focus on moving Divine energy into the body of the wand. Then sharply exhale through your nose, not your mouth. Do this at least three times, and for better results, nine times. Your pulsed breath and focused intention are the carrier waves that move the energy into the tool, consecrating it and making it sacred.

CASTING YOUR MAGIC CIRCLE

Within the magic circle, you can achieve a higher awareness, creating a connection to the Divine and Oneness. The circle is a vortex of light, setting up an energetic plane of communion between you and the Goddess and God. It also protects you from negative influences when you do magic.

You cast a magic circle every time you do magic. You will need a compass, athame, and a bowl with salt in it. First, use the compass to find North. Face North, and slowly spin in a clockwise circle, with your arms stretched outward. Imagine a clear blue light washing out the area as you say,

> *May all evil and foulness be gone from this place.*
> *I ask this in the Lady's name.*
> *Be gone, now and forevermore!*

Use your athame to draw a circle around your magic making area. To do this, point it at the North point. Imagine a blue-white flame coming out of the tip of the blade and creating a bright circle of light. If you don't have an athame, you can also use your wand or your dominant power hand (e.g., right if you are right-handed). Just imagine the light flaring from your wand tip or fingertips when you do this.

Next, purify the circle by taking a pinch of salt from the bowl, tossing it gently toward the North point, and say,

> *Ayea, Ayea Kerridwen!*
> *Ayea, Ayea Kernunnos!*
> *Ayea, Ayea, Ayea!*

If you prefer, you can use other Goddess and God names. I use the Celtic Mother Goddess and Father God because I have the strongest rapport with them. After purifying the North point, repeat this process for the East, South, and West points, in that order. At each point, sprinkle a pinch of salt, and repeat

> *Ayea, Ayea Kerridwen!*
> *Ayea, Ayea Kernunnos!*
> *Ayea, Ayea, Ayea!*

Then face the altar, and say in a firm voice,

> *I consecrate this circle of power to the Ancient Ones*
> *May they bless this circle with their presence.*
> *Blessed be! Blessed be all who are gathered here.*

When you are finished casting the circle, knock nine times on the altar with the base of your wand or your knuckles, in three series of three. Your circle is now set in place. While in the circle, always move clockwise, the direction of positivity in magic making.

CALLING IN THE ELEMENTAL POWERS

It is easy to call in the elemental powers to your circle. The reason for doing this is to set up a guardian at each of the elemental gates to protect your circle while you are doing magic. A different elemental guardian guards each of the gates or portals that lead to the Otherworld.

Once you set your circle in place, you call upon the elemental powers to stand guard at the threshold of each of the four corners. They remain there until you release them.

Facing your altar, and the North direction, stretch your arms toward the sky. Merge with the Earth element, and say,

> *Guardians of the North march,*
> *Generous powers of Earth,*
> *Protect the gate of the North ward,*
> *And guard this circle and all within.*
> *Come, I summon you!*

Now turn and face the East and stretch your arms toward the sky. Merge with the Air element, and say,

> *Guardians of the East march,*
> *Generous powers of Air,*
> *Protect the gate of the East ward,*
> *And guard this circle and all within.*
> *Come, I summon you!*

Then face the South, stretching your arms toward the sky, merge with the Fire element, and say,

> *Guardians of the South march,*
> *Generous powers of Fire,*
> *Protect the gate of the South ward,*
> *And guard this circle and all within.*
> *Come I summon you!*

Then face the West, and stretch your arms upward. Merging with the powers of Water, say,

> *Guardians of the West march,*
> *Generous powers of Water,*
> *Protect the gate of West ward,*

And guard this circle and all within.
Come, I summon you!

Now stand in the center of your magic circle, face your altar, and say,

Guardian spirits of Earth, Air, Fire, and Water
Grant me your power and protection tonight!

The elemental powers are now set in place.

CUTTING THE LITTLE GATE

Once you have called the elemental powers into the circle, you need to cut a "little gate." This gate is an energetic gate from which you can enter and exit without disrupting the magical energy of the circle. Cut this gate just below the East point of your circle either with your athame, holding it in your power hand, or with a sweeping gesture of your dominant hand. Just imagine cutting an energetic gate as you do this.

Open and close the little gate each time you enter and exit the circle by using your athame or a sweeping motion of your power hand. Whenever possible, I suggest that you cut the gate at the door, when working indoors, so you can easily come and go. Now that the circle is cast, it is time for you to make your magic potion or cast a magic spell. Please refer to chapters 4 and 5 for specific instructions. After you are done with your magic making, bid farewell to the elements and pull up the circle.

BIDDING FAREWELL TO THE ELEMENTS

Once the potion is made, the spell cast, or the ritual complete, it is time to bid farewell to the elements. To do this, begin at the North point, and say,

Generous powers of Earth, depart in peace.
Many thanks for your presence.

Then face East, and say,

> *Generous powers of Air, depart in peace.*
> *Many thanks for your presence.*

Next, turn to the South, and say,

> *Generous powers of Fire, depart in peace.*
> *Many thanks for your presence.*

Then face West, and say,

> *Generous powers of Water, depart in peace.*
> *Many thanks for your presence.*

PULLING UP THE MAGIC CIRCLE

After you have bid farewell to the elemental guardians, it is time to pull up the magic circle. Face North with your athame in your power hand pointed toward the North point of your magic circle. Slowly turn counterclockwise, and as you turn, imagine the blue-white light of the circle being drawn back into your athame. You can do this with your power hand or wand if you don't have an athame handy. After you are done pulling up the circle, knock three times on the altar with the base of your wand, or with the knuckles of your power hand.

3

Magical Timing

MAGICAL TIMING ADDS INCREDIBLE power to your work and increases your success rate. It is knowing the best hour, day, month, moon and sun phase to do magic. Timing helps make your magic flow, but it should not stop you from doing magic. For instance, the best time to make a love potion or cast a love spell for a new lover may be on a Friday, when the new moon is in Libra or Taurus, but what if you need to make the potion or cast the spell right now and can't wait until the timing is favorable? In that case, just time your magic the best you can, given the circumstances and time of day, week, month, and year.

Some witches and wizards learn the names and movements of the stars and planets, and the influences each has on magic. Rather than sending you out at night with your telescopes, this training guide simplifies the process by giving you easy-to-understand tables and lists on how the sun, moon, and planets affect magical timing. Remember timing is supposed to help you, not hinder you. So keep your focus, and above all, when doing any kind of magic, keep in mind that it's your intention and expectation going into the work that counts the most. Fully engage your senses and do what feels right. Trust your instincts and follow your intuitions.

MAGICAL HOURS OF THE DAY

An analogy of how the hours of the day influence magic can be drawn to a day in the life of a flower. With the first rays of sunshine, the flower begins to open. Then, it fully opens, and stays open until closing again at dusk. The flower quietly sleeps, yet it still continues to grow and develop all through the night, until the dawn comes once again.

Magical timing by the hour of the day follows the flower pattern. Although some of us are morning people, while others are night owls, you will discover that there are certain times during the day and night that you do your most successful magic. Pay attention to your own natural rhythms, and honor them, choosing the times when you have the most energy for magic making. The following is a table of correspondences for the daily timing of potions and spells.

DAWN

A time of renewal, rebirth, new ideas dawning, new beginnings, and consecration. Over the centuries, people have collected the dew on the grass and plants at dawn to use as a magic love potion.

MORNING

This is a good time for setting patterns in play, for preparing potions, and casting spells for attaining goals. The day's light is growing strong and your magic grows accordingly. Mid-morning is a good time to harvest flowers.

NOON

The solar energy is most powerful at high noon, and there is a tremendous amount of energy for magic making. Noon is also a good time to gather flowers for magical uses.

Afternoon

This is a time of harvesting magical goals. The heat of the afternoon sun is a good time for harvesting herbs for potions.

Dusk

A powerful junction point between solar and lunar energies, dusk is the time when the portals to all worlds are thrown open and you can freely enter them. This is a very potent time for any magic making because the portals are open and communication with Divine energies is particularly strong.

Dark of Night

The lunar and stellar energies are strongest at night. Throughout history, witches and wizards have almost always cast their spells under the cloak of night. This is also a good time to map out magical potions and spells.

Midnight

Traditionally called "the witching hour," midnight is a good time to let go of old habits or negative relationships and banish negativity from your life. This is also the time for updating your life patterns and practicing dream magic.

The Hour Before Dawn

This is the time of the Otherworld of faeries, and when many predators hunt. It is a good time to stay indoors.

NUMEROLOGY BY THE HOUR

Another more specific way to select the best hour of the day to make potions and cast spells is by using numerology. Each hour above 9:00

is added together. For example, 10 = 1 +0 = 1, or 12 = 1 + 2 = 3, and so forth. Eleven can be either 2 or 11, depending upon your intention. Obviously the hour number will be different if you are using military time. For example, 1:00 becomes 1300 hours in military time. The energies of 1 and 13 (1 + 3 = 4) do differ. I suggest you stick with one timing system, choosing the one that works best for you. The following is a listing of each hour number with its corresponding magical qualities.

1—Oneness, individuality, beginnings, initiation, creation
2—Partnership, balance of polarities, working with others
3—Divinity, magical power, the Otherworld, communication
4—Foundations, the four directions, construction, structure
5—Magic, travel, change, power, adventure, resourcefulness
6—Home, family, love, beauty, the creative arts, children
7—Wisdom, the seven chakras, birth, spirituality, faith
8—Reward, success, prosperity, the number of infinity, leadership
9—Compassion, tolerance, completion, knowledge
11—Intuition, spiritual healing, visions, psychic abilities
22—Mastery, mystery, rebirth, grand-scale networking

MAGICAL DAYS OF THE WEEK

Experienced witches and wizards know that Friday is the best day of the week to do love spells. Friday is named for Freya, the Norse Goddess of love, and it is also the day of the week ruled by the planet Venus, the Roman Goddess of love. Because of these Divine influences, the power of love is usually strong on Fridays.

Divine and astrological correspondences influence each day of the week, giving it certain energetic qualities. You can use these qualities to give rituals and spells an extra boost of energy and make potions more powerful. The following chart shows the days of the week, along with the types of potions, rituals, and spells, that work best on each day.

Monday—Moon's Day, ruled by the Moon
Potions, rituals, and spells for dreams, jobs, female fertility, psychic abilities, and beginning projects

Tuesday—Tyr's Day, ruled by Mars
Potions, rituals, and spells for courage, personal power, passion, business, conquering enemies, and to break negative spells

Wednesday—Woden's (Odin's) Day, ruled by Mercury
Potions, rituals, and spells for divination, wisdom, learning, creativity, communication, and psychic awareness

Thursday—Thor's Day, ruled by Jupiter
Potions, rituals, and spells for money, good luck, contracts, legal matters, expanding business, political power, and male fertility

Friday—Freya's Day, ruled by Venus
Potions, rituals, and spells for love, romance, friendship, happiness, beauty, musical skill, artistic ability, and sexuality

Saturday—Saturn's Day, ruled by Saturn
Potions, rituals, and spells for protection, property, inheritance, agriculture, life patterns, structure, and resolution

Sunday—Sun's Day, ruled by the Sun
Potions, rituals, and spells for healing, success, peace, harmony, and divine power

MAGICAL MONTHS AND MOONS

For thousands of years, witches and wizards have been using the energies of the sun, moon, and planets for magic making. You, too, can tap into these energies by properly timing your potions and spells. As mentioned previously, the energy is high for doing love magic on Fridays, especially on those Fridays when the full moon is in Libra or when the sun is Taurus. To find out what the exact sun and moon signs are for the days of the month, you can purchase an emphimerus or an astrology calendar at most New Age and witch and wizard shops.

For those of you who want to know more about astrology and how it influences magic, I recommend having your natal astrology chart done. Your natal chart is based on the date, time, and location of your birth. It shows where the sun, moon, and planets were positioned at the moment you were born. You can use your natal chart as a jumping-off point for making even more powerful potions and more successful spells. For now, apply the information in the following astrology table to your potions and spells to give them an extra boost of cosmic energy!

Aries (March 20 to April 19)
Fire power, building personal strength, adventuring, persisting, activating new ventures, stimulating moment, meeting challenges

Taurus (April 19 to May 20)
Creativity, love, fertility, security, sensual desire, determination, generating abundance, artistic inspiration, developing physical strength

Gemini (May 20 to June 21)
Balancing polarities, communication, ideas, curiosity, compromise, connecting with spirit guides, sending messages, developing psychic abilities

Cancer (June 21 to July 22)
Creating emotional balance, fertility, mothering, keeping secrets, protecting and blessing home and family, exploring past lives

Leo (July 22 to August 22)
Expressing yourself, building magical power, fathering, improving self-esteem, prowess, leadership, generosity, furthering your career, productivity

Virgo (August 22 to September 22)
Organizing, structuring, improving employment, working with others, healing, attending to details, analyzing, serving others

Libra (September 22 to October 23)

Discovering or enhancing romance, love, and relationships; balancing energies; creativity; making new friends and partnerships

Scorpio (October 23 to November 21/22)

Creativity, passion, shapeshifting, exploring mysteries, exploring past lives, moving past fear, inheritance, sex magic, divination

Sagittarius (November 21/22 to December 21)

Expanding knowledge, changing perceptions, being optimistic, traveling, changing bad luck to good luck, exploring new places and new ideas, going on vision quests

Capricorn (December 21 to January 19)

Practicality, discipline, giving order to your life, building ambition, developing patience, improving your public image, advancing your career, prosperity

Aquarius (January 19 to February 18)

Using astrological knowledge, stimulating action, mysticism, delving into the unknown, inventing new concepts and things, promoting change, working with groups

Pisces (February 18 to March 20)

Dream magic, enhancing intuition, connecting with the Divine, using your imagination, ancestral communication, increasing healing powers

MAGICAL MOON PHASES

Along with the tides, birth rates, and crimes of passion, the moon greatly affects your magical works. Each moon phase has its signature energy that influences the success of your potions, spells, and rituals. Your magical goals are much more likely to be attained if you coordinate them with the cycles of the moon.

Always consider the intent of the potion you are making, ritual you are performing, or spell you are spinning before deciding which moon phase will work best. The phase of the moon that you do your magic in depends upon your goal. Remember if you need to do a magical work immediately because of a pressing situation, time things out the best you can. For example, if the moon phase isn't conducive for doing a love spell, focus instead on the best hour of the day when your personal energy is at its highest. The following list of moon phases and their suggested magical uses, can be used to empower your magic making.

New Moon (night of the new moon)
A good time to initiate new beginnings, new jobs, new relationships, new ventures, and new ideas.

Waxing Crescent Moon (first seven days after the new moon)
A good time to create growth, protect animals, make changes, make new associations, and get help with business affairs.

Waxing Moon (seven to ten days after the new moon)
A good time to form new friendships, work on creative efforts, move forward, attract prosperity, and increase good luck.

Gibbous Moon (ten to thirteen days after the new moon)
A good time for divination, to do love and prosperity spells, attract friends, completing magical goals, personal growth, and developing patience.

Full Moon (night of the full moon)
A good time for handfastings, enhancing your love life, being more creative, doing dream magic; divination, scrying, and developing your healing abilities. Do spells and make potions for fertility, prosperity, dreams, inspiration, and intuition. The full moon, also called the High Moon by witches and wizards, has the strongest lunar energy and is a great time for doing all kinds of positive magic.

Waning Gibbous (the seven days that follow a full moon)
A good time to rid yourself of negative relationships, addictions, and habits.

Waning Crescent (seven days after the full moon to the new moon)
A good time to rid or remove something or someone negative from your life, to overcome obstacles, and build your powers of protection.

Dark or Black Moon (no visible moon)
A good time to protect yourself from negativity and negative works, do invisibility spells, meditate, dissolve ties, and finish pending business.

MAGICAL MOON ESBATS

Witches and wizards call the thirteen moons every year the Esbats. Just like the moon phases, the Esbats all have signature energies. Each Esbat has a magical name and has innate qualities for making certain kinds of potions and spinning particular spells. For example, the Hare Moon is an especially fertile time, while the Snow Moon is the perfect time for freezing any negativity out of your life.

To know which Esbat matches which moon name, start counting the moons, beginning with the first full moon after the Winter Solstice (usually on December 21 or 22). For example, if a full moon rises on December 24 in a given year, it would be the first Esbat called the Wolf Moon. You can check an emphimerus or astrology calendar for the exact date of the Winter Solstice and each of the full moons. The following table lists the Esbats, their magical names, and their magic making qualities.

1st Esbat   Wolf Moon
Personal potential, loyalty, the family, trusting your instincts, developing clairvoyance, lucid dreams

2nd Esbat   Storm Moon
Polarities, duality, creating intensity, purification, getting rid of bad habits

3rd Esbat   Chaste Moon
Purity, natural balance, the trinity of Maid/Mother/Crone and Son/Father/Wise Man

4th Esbat   Seed Moon
Planting seeds for attaining your magical goals, using the power of the four elements

5th Esbat   Hare Moon
Balancing your ego, improving your physical environment, fertility, advancing toward your magical goals

6th Esbat   Dyad Moon
Bridging the divine and mundane, shapeshifting, Divine gifts, personal growth

7th Esbat   Mead Moon
Altered states of awareness, lucid dreaming, Divine communication, personal fluorescence

8th Esbat   Wort Moon
The cycles of things, putting ideas together, cultivating well-thought out magical patterns

9th Esbat   Barley Moon
Increasing personal will, honing skills, attaining magical goals

10th Esbat   Wine Moon
Healing, divination, developing psychic abilities, Divine inspiration, healing power

11th Esbat   Blood Moon
Ancestral communion, maternity, paternity, fellowship, divine oaths

12th Esbat   Snow Moon
Focusing on the Divine within, change, freezing out negativity

13th Esbat   Oak Moon
Rebirth, metamorphosis, transformation, incarnation, transmigration

Magical Sun Sabbats

Witches and wizards celebrate eight sun Sabbats, also called the Quarter (the solstices and equinoxes) and Cross-Quarter Days (the four days that fall halfway between the solstices and equinoxes). The eight Sabbats follow the path of the sun through the seasons. In traditional practice, they are exactly at 00.00 degrees and 15.00 degrees of the astrological sun sign they fall under. In modern practice, the Sabbats each have a set date. I have listed both the astrological degrees and exact dates for your reference.

The eves of each of the Sabbats are the best times for witches and wizards to do all kinds of magic because the universal energy is at its peak. The following table lists the Sabbats and their corresponding dates and magical qualities.

Winter Solstice
Also called Yule (Quarter)
00.00 degrees Capricorn
Date: December 21 or 22
Magical Qualities: Associated with the rebirth and blessings of the sun. A time of letting the past go, of reflection, and building personal strength, protection, and integration.

Imbolc
Also called Bridget's Fire and Candlemas (Cross-Quarter)
15.00 degrees Aquarius
Date: February 2
Magical Qualities: Associated with the sacred fire, which can be used to rekindle your magical goals. A good time to start projects and think about what it is you really want to create in your life.

Spring Equinox

Also called Hertha's Day and Ostara (Quarter)

00.00 degrees Aries

Date: March 21 or 22

Magical Qualities: A time of planting seeds and ideas, of fertility, of combining elements, and bridging obstacles. The perfect time for learning from nature.

Beltane

Also called May Day (Cross-Quarter)

15.00 degrees Taurus

Date: May 1

Magical Qualities: A time of youth and playfulness, sexuality, increasing fertility, union, and romance. One of the prime Sabbats with lots of delightful energy for magic making of all kinds!

Summer Solstice

Also called Midsummer and Letha's Day (Quarter)

00.00 degrees Cancer

Date: June 21 or 22

Magical Qualities: A time of absolute florescence, of honoring the ancestors and the faeries. A good day for forming new alliances with Otherworldly beings and creatures, for shapeshifting, and working with your power animals.

Lughnassad

Also called Lammas (Cross-Quarter)

15.00 degrees Leo

Date: First week of August

Magical Qualities: A time for mastering skills, learning new things, joining together, handfastings, and beginning to harvest your goals.

Autumnal Equinox

Also called Hellith's Day and Mabon (Quarter)

00.00 degrees Libra

Date: September 21 or 22

Magical Qualities: A pivotal point when personal goals come to fruition as well as the time for setting up new patterns for the future.

Samhain

Also called Halloween, Hallowmass, All Hallow's Eve (Cross-Quarter)

15.00 degrees Scorpio

Date: October 31

Magical Qualities: When the veil between the worlds is at its thinnest. One of the prime Sabbats for doing all kinds of magic, including shapeshifting, astral travel, ancestral communion, honoring the dead, and working with the faeries.

4

Magic Potions

Brewing potions for magic making is easy and a lot of fun. The art of brewing potions is thousands of years old, and still evolving. Making magic potions is basic training for all witches and wizards. Mixing them and getting them to work in a magical sense is the trick. This training guide integrates both traditional and modern techniques for doing just that!

The magic potion recipes in this chapter include a list of ingredients, as well as instructions on how to prepare and take the potion. At the end of the potion recipes (page 86) is a listing of basic potion ingredients. This way, you can both vary the potions in this book by adding ingredients, or when you become adept at the techniques, create potions of your own.

As with anything dealing with chemistry, potions require a little common sense when mixing different ingredients together. Each ingredient adds to the overall whole. This means you don't want to add anything that doesn't work within terms of the whole. Use ingredients that have properties that match your magical goal, and make sure you know exactly how you want to use the potion before preparing it.

There is some controversy between experienced witches and wizards as to whether students of magic should make up their own potion recipes. Some feel that you should follow a recipe exactly as it is written, and never get creative because potions are an area of magic that should be approached with extreme caution. Other teachers advocate a much more open approach; after the student learns a particular potion and its effect, it's a good time to experiment by adding or subtracting ingredients, and thus altering the overall effect of the potion.

I think it is important to first learn how to make potions by following the recipes exactly as they are noted. As with many subjects, it is important to learn the *techniques* for making magic potions, and to learn how the ingredients *work together* before running off and trying to make potions of your own.

If you do begin making potions of your own, I suggest that you use an already existing potion recipe, and then modify it slightly by adding a safe ingredient that you know will improve the potion. Notice what effect this new ingredient has on the quality of the potion. Take it one step at a time, adding or subtracting an ingredient, and then check the effect the new ingredient has on the overall effect of the potion.

By learning the magical qualities of each ingredient, you have an idea of what will and what won't work before you even put the ingredient in the potion. Either way, you should always test your potion after altering its recipe. Be cautious and never use ingredients that are poisonous or can cause harm to yourself or anyone else.

Funk and Wagnall's *Standard College Dictionary* defines a potion as "a large dose of liquid medicine" that is "often used as a magic or poisonous draft." This guide explores the magical uses of potions but does not delve into their poisonous or negative applications. In a traditional sense, a potion is a concoction of herbs or other ingredients that have been steeped in water for beneficial magical purposes. For example, love potions can add to a person's overall happiness and well-being which is, without a doubt, beneficial.

According to modern witches and wizards, a potion is usually a mixture of ingestible ingredients such as herbal teas or fruit drinks that can be used specifically in magic making, and are consumed.

Also, there are potion powders, waters, and other miscellaneous con-coctions, all under the umbrella name of "magic potions." Beware, many of these potions are not consumed.

In magic making, potions can be used alone or in spell casting. To work as they are intended and to give them magical energies, potions should be made during the appropriate phase of the moon and on the most appropriate day. (Please refer to chapter 3, "Magical Timing," for tables of correspondences.)

THE MANY MAGICAL USES OF POTIONS

Mythology, faery tales, books, and movies, all brim with stories of witches and wizards standing over a steaming cauldron brewing potions and chanting incantations over their heady mixtures. The Harry Potter books by J. K. Rowling, other literary sources as diverse as the Bible, Shakespeare's play, *A Midsummer Night's Dream*, and Walt Disney's film, *The Sword and the Stone*, all contain references to potions and their many uses, from love and romance to turning the bad guys into toads. For example, when speaking of a love attraction potion in Shakespeare's *A Midsummer Night's Dream*, Oberon says to Puck, "Fetch me that flower; the herb I shew'd thee once; The juice of it on sleeping eye-lids laid; Will make a man or woman madly dote; Upon the next live creature that it sees."

According to ancient magical texts, there are potions for just about everything you can imagine. With the right magic potion, you can become invisible, stay forever young, or fly through the air. You can brew a potion for glory or bottle fame.

Unfortunately, those misdirected witches and wizards who practice the Dark Arts also use potions to hurt, control, or destroy people that get in the way of Darkness's quest for absolute power and its destruc-tion of light. With your magic, you can make the mountains sing, or the ancient ones cry, so be sure to do only positive magic as your negative works will eventually come back and destroy you.

Historically, witches, wizards, druids, and shamans were the knowledge keepers for a particular tribe of people. This knowledge included everything from knowing which herbs to use when someone was sick to invoking Divine energy to make the crops grow strong. Even today in the age of synthetic drugs that are used to treat everything imaginable, most synthetic medicines are artificial replications of natural herbs and potions used by witches and wizards for thousands of years. A classic example is aspirin, used by healers since its original marketing in the 1800s. It is a synthetic duplicate of a natural herbal potion made from white willow bark that has been used for years by mystical practitioners to ease pain.

Because they were the keepers of knowledge, witches and wizards were our first astronomers, healers, priests, and priestesses. They carried a body of practical knowledge that was passed down through generations from teacher to student in a training that was secret and transmitted orally rather than in written form. It is a knowledge that has been added to and fine-tuned by each succeeding generation. Making magic potions is one of these traditions passed down through time.

MAGIC CAULDRONS

Merlin was one of the most famous wizards of all time. He excelled at making magic potions. Like the Norse God Odin, Merlin's main quest was knowledge, and he learned all there was about potions. In the popular comic strip *The Wizard of Id*, whose main character is based on Merlin, the wizard is almost always making a magic potion in his large black cauldron over the fire. It is but one example of the close association that cauldrons have with the art and craft of making magic potions.

One of the most famous magic cauldrons mentioned in mythology is that of the Gaelic God Dagda, who as king of the gods was known as the "Good God." His cauldron had the power to bring the dead back to life, heal wounds, and provide unlimited food and drink. Dagda's Cauldron plays an important part in Celtic mythology, and in later retelling, the cauldron becomes the Holy Grail of Christ.

You can still get an old-fashioned cast iron witch's and wizard's cauldron for magic making, but I wouldn't suggest brewing too many of your potions in it because its metallic qualities can adversely alter the potion. More often than not, today's cauldrons take the shape of ceramic teapots (the kind that strain the contents from the liquid as it is poured), earthenware pots, crock pots, blenders, clear glass jars, and colored glass containers. I don't suggest using microwaves ovens when making potions as they rob the ingredients of essential nutrients. Although the items for making magic potions have changed through the ages, the techniques are basically the same. With a bit of effort and concentration, you will find that potions can really add power to your magic.

BASIC POTION INGREDIENTS

The basic ingredients used in making potions can be either gathered, grown, or purchased. Some of the ingredients, such as unicorn horns, snake fangs, black beetle eyes, leeches, and belladonna, mentioned in fictional stories are things you do not want to include in any of your magic potions, because as with unicorn horns, you may not only have problems finding the ingredient, but some are poisonous such as the herb belladonna. On the other side, ingredients such as nettles and wormwood are ingredients that could wind up in a magic potion.

It is important for you to be aware of the qualities of the ingredients you put in a potion, particularly one you've never tried before. Each ingredient has a magical quality that makes it useful. Many of these qualities are traditional. For example, to strengthen their memory, students in ancient Greece used rosemary herb twined in their hair or crushed it in bowls and kept it nearby while studying for examinations. Wizards use potions made from the herb valerian root to raise and commune with spirits. The Jicarilla Apache call sage "ghost medicine," and say brushing the body with it drives away bad dreams and nightmares. All of these uses point to a common theme— for thousands of years people all over the world have been using herbs in magical ways.

Through our senses, nature communicates her power directly through color, smell, taste, sound, shape, and texture, as well as other more subtle energies. By watching animals, we discovered the healing and magical qualities of plants. Over the years and through generations, people of all cultures now know that herbs, flowers, fruits, barks, fungi, and other plants are very effective in enhancing our bodies, minds, and spirits. Today, more and more people are getting back in touch with the magical qualities of plants by taking herbal supplements and drinking herbal teas, as well as consuming more fresh fruits and vegetables.

By combining certain herbs and other ingredients, your magic potions can be used for many practical things, from making you more creative and stimulating your senses, to bringing more love and prosperity into your life. Their magical power is waiting to be utilized by you, the practitioner.

HARVESTING MAGICAL INGREDIENTS

You can purchase all the ingredients you need to make potions from the market, or better yet, you can grow them yourself. This enhances their magical energy enormously because you can strengthen their energy by working with them. For example, when you hold seeds in your hands before planting, empower them with bright light. When you plant the seeds, imagine all of the fabulous magical goals that you are planting, and how powerful the plants will be when they grow tall and strong. When you water the seeds and later the plants, imagine the water energizing them even more. And when you har-

vest the plants, do so in a magical and respectful way. This will make
their power even stronger. Right after the plant is freshly harvested is
the best time to use it for magic because its power is the strongest.

If you are not able to grow the ingredients for your potions, then
the next best thing to do is to gather them from nature. When doing
this, make sure you know what you are gathering. Some things like
lavender or sage are fairly obvious, even to the novice, but other ingredients such as mugwort and catnip may not be readily identifiable.

If you are going to be using fresh plants, you can harvest them
whenever you like, depending upon your magical goal. (Please refer
to the "Magical Timing" section in chapter 3.) But if you are going
to be drying the herbs for later use, be sure to pick them after the
morning dew has dried, or else they will be more prone to molding.

Gather flowers for potions and spells when they first open, which
is when their fragrance is sweet, and their magical power the
strongest. You can also pick flowers when they are fully opened, usually by noontime, when their energy peaks. It's best to gather roots
once the plant passes into dormancy. Bark can be collected any time,
but remember it takes a long time to completely dry out before you
can grind it up. The eight Sabbats are the best times to gather bark.

When you harvest a plant, either mentally think to it or talk to it
out loud, and tell it exactly what you will be using it for. Then thank
the plant. Use your bolline, athame, or fingers to carefully break the
pieces off that you will need for magic making. Avoid taking more
that you need. To assure continued growth of the plant, never take all
the plants from any one area if you are gathering them in nature.
Quite often, you only need a small piece of the plant, for example
one rose or a few pieces of oak bark. When you take pieces, do so
gently, with respect.

After harvesting the plant, I suggest you leave a gift for it, either at
the base of the plant or in the area it grew. This can include a small
white stone, a sea shell, seeds, a flower, bulbs, rooted cuttings, a
feather, a song, or a simple prayer for the plant's continued existence.

MAKING MAGIC POTIONS

The art of making potions goes back to the earliest civilizations and in terms of history, as one of the oldest crafts known to humankind. Brewing beer, making wine, and infusing potions are traditions that have been perfected through time. Many of the techniques for making a great beer, wine, or potion are the same. The mixture is often called a wort. The wort is then put through a process, which in the case of potions, gives it magical properties.

The different ways of making potions stem from ancient medicinal and alchemical recipes, formulas that you can put together from basic ingredients in the privacy of your own kitchen. Historically magic love potions, also called philters, were often made of unappealing ingredients. You had to be extremely thirsty or unaware of the contents to sip one. Today, this isn't the case as most potion ingredients are tasty and appealing.

Potion brews can be anything from an herb tea to a fruit smoothie. One of the main things to remember when making any potion is to make it taste good if a person is going to drink it. If you are using a potion primarily for its scent, for example in a powder form, then make sure it smells good. Try to avoid unfortunate situations like the infamous wizard Aleister Crowley found himself in when he developed a perfume potion for sex magic called "It." Great idea Aleister, but nothing came of "It," because the stuff reputedly had a horrid smell!

Before you make your potion, be sure that you have all the ingredients and tools you will need at your fingertips. Following is a list of potion-making tools you will need:

- A ceramic, earthenware, glass, or wood bowl
- A pot, preferably one that is NOT made of metal, for brewing the potion
- A wooden spoon for stirring the potion
- Cheesecloth for straining the potion

- A mortar and pestle for grinding potion ingredients
- A container for the potion

Clean, preferably sterilize, all of your tools, especially the potion container. You can clean containers by carefully pouring boiling water into them, or you can put the container in the dishwasher, running it through the entire cycle and turning on the heat/dry cycle. This also does a good job of sterilizing containers. If you don't have time to properly clean the chalice, cup, glass, or other container the potion is going in, then just make sure that it is as clean as possible. Any residue may taint the potion.

The kind of water you use is important when preparing a magic potion. Spring, well, rain, and distilled waters are better than tap water, which often contains chemicals such as chlorine and fluoride. Well water with no harmful contaminants can be used; rain water can be used as long as there aren't any pollutants in it; and distilled water can be used for potions, but it is inert. Unless the recipe calls for it, I seldom use sea water or mineral water due to their mineral content.

Witches and wizards make potions by mixing one, two, a few, or many ingredients together into one. Sometimes the ingredients are used just as they are. Other times they are ground up, shredded, puréed, or crushed with your fingers or with the mortar and pestle. The herbs that go into your potion can be either fresh or dried. If you use fresh herbs, it takes three times more of them than dried herbs. For example, if a potion recipe calls for one teaspoon of dried sage leaves and you want to use fresh sage, it would take three teaspoons of fresh sage to make the potion.

Processes called infusions and decoctions are also employed. An infusion, the most common method of internal herbal preparation, is usually in the form of a tea. It can also take the form of a magic water. The infusion method works best when the potion you are making requires soft plant parts, such as leaves, flowers, or green stems.

When using the infusion method of preparing potions, there are a couple of things you can do to make your potion more effective. One thing is to brew aromatic ingredients, such as garlic and clove, in a pot with a lid that fits on tight. The reason for this is to keep from losing the natural oils of the aromatic ingredient to evaporation. These natural oils are important for the effectiveness of the potion.

Some ingredients are sensitive to heat, so you can make a cold infusion by soaking the herbs in water for anywhere from 6 to 12 hours. A sealed earthenware pot is best for cold infusions. When preparing potions using the infusion method, only make enough for immediate use as infusions rapidly lose their potency.

The method for making a decoction potion is similar to the infusion. You begin by grinding your ingredients into a powder that you can then use to make your potions. Ingredients that are hard, such as bark and stems, require more heat to release their magical properties. This use of more heat to release the natural oils of an ingredient is the primary difference between the infusion and decoction methods of potion making.

The decoction method would be the one most associated with the traditional use of magic cauldrons. In this way, dried herbal ingredients are ground into powder and are cut into small pieces, and then added to the potion. The potion is made in a pot, and the ingredients are simmered and boiled in order to release their magical properties. Again in the case of aromatic ingredients, you should use a lid on the pot to slow the evaporation process. The amount of time that you heat the mixture depends on the potion recipe. Usually decoctions are strained to eliminate the hard bark and stems before using them.

At times, potions use both methods in their recipe. In this case prepare the two separately as a decoction and infusion, and then mix the ingredients together after the decoction has cooled. By doing so, the infusion ingredients are not ruined by the heat that the decoction process requires. Always stir clockwise.

MAGIC POWDER POTIONS

Magic powder potions are easy to make as most of them require no cooking. Make these by finely grinding up the ingredients listed in the powder potion recipes. Use your mortar and pestle and also your fingers to crush the ingredients. The whole time you are grinding the ingredients, focus on your magical goal as it is essential to empower the ingredients. Always grind clockwise.

You can also purchase ingredients that are already ground up. If you do so, be sure to get in touch with the ingredients by running them through your fingers as you concentrate on empowering them. See and sense the magic powder potion working exactly the way you intended.

To use the magic powder potion, simply sprinkle it to release its power. As you are sprinkling it, be sure to focus on your magical goal. You can sprinkle magic powder potions in a clockwise circle around you, beginning and ending in the North, or you can sprinkle the powder in certain magical shapes, for example, a love powder can be sprinkled in a heart shape. You can also sprinkle magic potion powders on your altar, around altar candles, and on crystals and gemstones. Again, it's your intent and focus as you empower the potion ingredients and sprinkle them that really gets the magic flowing.

EMPOWERING YOUR MAGIC POTION

As mentioned previously, to empower or enchant magic potions, focus your mind on your magical goal and on the specific effect you expect the potion to have. Use your intention plus the natural energy of the ingredients to cook the magical energy into them. Your focused energy is imparted into the ingredients through your willful intent, your touch, and the heat of your hands.

Use the three basic steps of magic—intention coupled with expectation, desire, and merging—to empower the potion. When you mix the ingredients, mix them with the intention and expectation of imparting your magical goal into them.

You can also use the power of touch to enchant potion ingredients. First, wash your hands well, dry them, and then rub the palms of your hands briskly together to charge them with energy. Immediately place your hands on the ingredients for a few moments, imagining that you are transferring the energy in your hands into the potion ingredients, very much like you would bless food. Then, whenever possible, use the fingers of your power hand to mix the ingredients. Your power hand is your right hand if you are right-handed, your left if you are left-handed. If you are ambidextrous, your power hand is the one you eat with. If you are using a wooden spoon or blender to mix the ingredients, visualize or sense the energy from your hands moving into the spoon or blender, and then moving into the potion mixture. If you need to, just pretend doing this at first until you get the hang of it.

While you mix and charge the potion ingredients, either with your fingers, a wooden spoon, or in a blender, send your energy into the mixture. The stronger your desire for your goal, the stronger the energy you impart into the potion. At first it may seem odd to actually be sending power or energy into the ingredients, but with a little practice, empowering and energetically charging potions becomes a natural skill that is easy and fun. You will also begin to understand how powerful transferring energy from your hands to another object, or from your mind to a specific goal, can really be. More specifically, how this energy can be applied toward attaining your magical goals.

The key to empowering potions, as in all magical work, is to stay focused on your magical goal for the entire time it takes to make and use the potion. For example, if you are adding the ingredients of vanilla or honey to a love potion, concentrate on each ingredient bringing sweet and delicious love into your life. See, touch, taste, hear, and smell the love coming into your life. Imagine the potion being particularly effective. See and sense it as already having the proper effect. Do this by moving your awareness into the near future, and imagining the successful effect of the potion. In your awareness, feel the great joy and happiness of having the potion work, of attaining your magical goal. See and sense your magical success. Bathe in the glow of energy that surrounds it.

Then move your awareness back to the present, and impart that image and joyful energy, that great feeling, into the potion ingredients. You can do this by imagining a bright white light coming from your hands and moving into the ingredients, or you can see and sense a laser beam of light coming from your third eye (on your forehead between your eyebrows) and igniting the ingredients with its powerful radiance. You can also use deep breathing to empower potions by sensing yourself breathing bright energy into the ingredients.

After you have placed the potion in its container, you can empower it even more by saying something like,

> *Magic powers that be*
> *Please bless this potion*
> *On earth, sky, and sea*
> *Charge it with Divine power*
> *So be it! Blessed be!*

NINE EASY STEPS FOR MAKING A MAGIC POTION

1. Gather together all the ingredients you will need to make the potion. Light a candle if you like, matching its color and dedication to your potion's purpose. Be sure to place your candle(s) near your working surface as a focusing tool, but not in the way.
2. Draw a magic circle around your working area. For example, if you are working in the kitchen, draw a magic circle around the entire room.

3. Call in the elemental powers to your circle. A shorthand method for doing this is by saying something like:

> "I ask that the generous powers of earth, air, fire, and water come into this circle. Come I pray you!"

4. Call in spirit, the Divine, into your circle by saying something like:

> "May the Divine Ones enter into this circle and bless this potion with their Divine power."

5. Next, empower the potion ingredients.
6. Make the potion.
7. Empower the potion once more with a magical incantation, and then use it *immediately* as suggested.
8. Thank the elements and spirit.
9. Pull up the magic circle and put everything away.

MAGIC POTIONS RECIPES

These easy-to-prepare recipes provide suggested proportions and can be adjusted depending upon the ingredients available and personal preference. For example, if you want to make a love potion with strawberries in it, and you know the person that will be drinking it is allergic to strawberries, then substitute an ingredient that will create the same basic effect. In this case, you could substitute peaches or raspberries for strawberries.

You can drink some of the potions, whereas others you sprinkle or sniff. If you are drinking the potion, I suggest that you make an appropriate toast before doing so. For example, if it's a love potion, say something like: "May our love blossom with this magic love potion."

I also suggest you keep track of the changes you make to potions, and their effects, either in the margins of this book, in a notebook, or on index cards. I sincerely hope that these magic potion recipes will help you on your quest to become successful modern witches and wizards. May the magic forever live within us all. It's what makes life extraordinary!

Love Potions

In the classic pop song "Love Potion #9," the singer of the song goes to see a gypsy with a gold-capped tooth in order to improve his love life. She mixes up a potion in her kitchen sink that smells like turpentine and looks like India ink. After drinking it, the singer kisses everything in sight until he kisses a policeman, who breaks his bottle of "Love Potion #9," thus ending the power of the potion.

With the proper empowerment, the following love potion recipes can be used to get your love life cooking. The first potion, Love Potion #9, uses the passion of fruits and traditional love inducers such as rose petals and vanilla to lure that perfect lover into your life. And I guarantee it tastes nothing like turpentine!

LOVE POTION #9

1 cup crushed ice (fill your blender about ¼ full)	½ ripe banana
½ cup papaya nectar	¼ cup strawberries
⅛ cup pineapple juice	¼ cup peach juice
¼ cup orange juice	3 rose petals
	3 drops of vanilla

In a blender, blend all the ingredients at high speed until smooth.

Makes two servings, one for your intended love, and one for you. Slowly sip the potion together.

Venus Water

1 cup water
3 roses

Pull off the rose petals, one at a time, all the while empowering them, and then put them in a pot with the water. Simmer slowly for about 15 to 20 minutes, then let the liquid cool. Strain the water, and put it in a container. Sprinkle it in your bedroom, on your person, around your working space, in your car, or anyplace where you would like to encourage more love. There is an old folk belief that if you rinse your hands with Venus Water before mixing a love potion, the potion will be more effective.

True Love Potion

4 cups water
4 bags of rose hips tea
½ teaspoon catnip
¼ teaspoon pure vanilla

A small pinch of crushed
   rosemary
1 teaspoon honey

Boil the water and steep the tea bags for about 8 minutes. Add the catnip, vanilla, rosemary. Let it steep for another 5 minutes. Strain the tea, heat it, and sweeten with the honey. This potion works best if sipped together while gazing into one another's eyes. Inspires tenderness, fidelity, and feelings of love and romance.

Makes four servings, two for you and two for your intended love

June Bride Potion

1 cup tomato juice
1 bay leaf (crushed)
3 dashes of dill

3 dashes celery salt
3 pinches of basil

Put all of the ingredients in a pot and simmer the brew for 5 minutes. Chill completely, then strain the potion and serve. Be certain you are ready for the effect, which can often be a proposal of marriage.

Makes one serving

Full Moon Love Potion

3 cups boiling water
A pinch of cumin
A pinch of rosemary
A pinch of thyme
3 pinches of dried mint leaves (6 pinches of fresh mint leaves)

3 dashes of nutmeg
1 teaspoon dried lemon peel
1 teaspoon orange peel
5 rose petals
3 teaspoons of black tea
3 teaspoons honey

Put all the ingredients, except the honey, into a ceramic teapot or the like, and then carefully pour the boiling water into the teapot. Add honey and serve it to your intended lover. Sip the potion together slowly while watching the full moon rise. In the summertime and in hot climates, you can chill the potion and serve over ice.

Makes three cups

Midsummer's Eve Magic Potion

2 cups boiling water
3 chamomile tea bags
6 rose petals
1 pinch lavender
1 clove

A dash of nutmeg
½ teaspoon fresh crushed
ginger (a dash of dried
ginger)

This one is especially effective when prepared on Midsummer's Eve. Put all the ingredients into a ceramic teapot and carefully pour the boiling water over them. Serve warm or chilled.

Makes about two cups

Attraction Potion

½ cup apricot juice
½ cup orange juice
1 cup apple juice

A sprig of mint or a small
pinch of dried mint

Mix the juices together in a large glass or ceramic pitcher. Pour into two glasses (over ice if you like) and garnish with the mint. Serve immediately.

Makes two servings

Endless Romantic Potion

1 cup boiling water
1 chamomile tea bag
1 peppermint tea bag

½ teaspoon lemon juice
1 cup apple juice

Put the tea bags into the cup of boiling water and let them steep for 20 minutes. Fill two glasses with ½ cup tea, and then add ½ cup apple juice to each. Put ¼ teaspoon lemon juice in each glass, and stir thoroughly. Chill and serve. This potion works best when sipped together with the person you want to romance.

Makes two cups

Be My Valentine Potion

2 cups milk
1 teaspoon sweetened cocoa
A dash of cinnamon

A few drops of vanilla
9 marshmallows

Heat the milk slowly, stirring in each of the ingredients. Add the marshmallows last. With each marshmallow you put into the potion, imagine your Valentine being yours and feeling divine! Pour into cups and sip together with your Valentine.

Makes two cups

IN LOVE AND LUST POTION

4 ripe pears, peeled   1 nickel-sized piece of peeled
6 Red Delicious apples,   ginger (optional)
  peeled

Make this potion just prior to using it. First remove the core and seeds from the apples and pears. Next, cut the fruit into small pieces and put the pieces through a juicer along with the ginger. Drink the potion with your lover to stimulate romance, love, and passion.

Makes two servings

FRIENDSHIP POTION

1 cup lemon-lime soda   2 slices of lemon
1 cup strawberry or apricot
  juice

In two glasses, pour equal parts of the soda and juice, and garnish each glass with a slice of lemon. Drink this potion with new friends.

Makes two servings

POTIONS FOR EMPOWERMENT

The following potion recipes can be used to empower you. You can take them as often as you like.

SUNSHINE POTION

A cup water
Sunshine

Set a covered clear glass container filled with the cup of water outside at dawn where it can soak up the rays of the morning sun. Do this with the expectation that Divine power of the sun will be imparted into the water. Then move it around a few times during the day so it can soak up as much direct sunlight as possible. Each time you do this, do so with expectation, once again focusing on strengthening the solar power within the potion. Just before the sun sets, bring the potion inside. You can either drink the sunshine potion immediately, or put in your bath that same night to fill you full of sunshine and bright energy.

Makes one cup

FULL MOON POTION

A cup water
A full moon

Set a covered clear glass jar filled with the cup of water out at night just as the full moon rises. Position the jar so that the water can soak in the moon rays all night. About one hour before dawn, go outside and bring the potion indoors. Drink the water immediately to increase your psychic awareness and powers of intuition.

Makes one cup

MAGIC POWER POTION

⅛ cup chilled pineapple
  juice
¼ cup chilled grape juice
⅛ cup ice water

½ cup chilled raspberries or
  strawberries
1 cup raspberry or strawberry
  yogurt

In a blender, combine all the ingredients. Blend until the potion is thick and smooth. All the while you are blending it, focus on feeling more energized and powerful.

Makes two servings

MEMORY POTION

1 cup boiling water
A pinch of rosemary
A pinch of rose petals

A pinch of mint
A pinch of sage
1 bay leaf (crushed)

Put all the ingredients, except the water into a cup. Carefully pour the boiling water into the cup, cover it, and let the brew steep for a few minutes. Anoint your body with the potion and add it to your bath water while imagining your memory becoming sharper and stronger. You can also sprinkle the potion on tools, pens and pencils, around your working area, or even rub a little on your computer while concentrating on your magical goal.

CREATIVITY POTION

½ cup crushed ice
1 cup papaya nectar
¼ cup pineapple juice

½ ripe banana
¼ cup raspberry or blackberry juice

Blend all the ingredients in a blender, until the mixture is smooth.

Makes two servings

IMMORTALITY POTION

2 cups apple cider
¼ cup cranberry juice
3 teaspoons brown sugar or honey

1 cinnamon stick
3 orange slices, peeled
3 whole cloves

Put the cider, cranberry juice, brown sugar, cinnamon stick in a crockpot or similar pot. Push the cloves into the orange slices, one clove per slice, and put the slices into the mixture. Warm the potions in the crockpot. Pour into a mug. As you are sipping the brew, imagine yourself living a long and healthy life. Move your mind into the future, and see the images of you growing old. Then move that energy into the potion using your will, focused breathing, and the heat of your hands as you hold the mug.

Makes two servings

POWER DREAMING POTION

1 cup boiling water
1 rose hips tea bag
A dash of cinnamon

A pinch of lavender
1 teaspoon honey

Put all the ingredients in a cup and pour the boiling water over them. Stir well, cover the mixture, and let it steep for 5 minutes. Drink just before going to sleep to induce psychic dreams.

Makes one serving

PLEASANT DREAMS POTION

3 cups water
⅓ cup rose petals

1 pinch cinnamon
3 bay leaves (crushed)

Do not drink this potion. It works by being inhaled slowly. Put all the ingredients into a teapot or pot with a lid. Pour the boiling water over the ingredients and cover the pot for five minutes. Take the covered pot into your bedroom. Put it on a sturdy surface, and then take off the cover. Carefully inhale the steam for a few minutes. Be very careful because the steam is hot. Leave the cover off and let the aroma fill your bedroom. Lay down and drift to sleep with the expectation of having pleasant dreams.

BRIGHT BLESSINGS POTION

½ cup orange juice
½ cup fat-free sweetened
   condensed milk

1 ripe banana
¼ cup club soda
4 ice cubes

As you put each of the ingredients, one by one, into the blender,
empower them with the blessings of the Goddess and God. You can
do this by simply dedicating each ingredient to a favorite Divine
presence. Blend all the ingredients until the potion is thick and
smooth. As you slowly sip the potion, think of all the blessings in
your life such as the people who love you and the many opportuni-
ties you have been given. Feel the joy of these blessings coursing
through you as you drink the potion.

Makes one large serving

ALL HALLOW'S EVE POTION

2 cups apple cider
2 pieces of candied ginger
   (or a dash of ginger and a
   dash of brown sugar)

1 cinnamon stick
2 whole cloves

Tie the ginger, cinnamon stick, and cloves in a piece of cheesecloth.
Warm the cider and spice pouch in a ceramic pot over low heat. Be
careful not to boil the potion. Before drinking, remove the spice
pouch, and pour the mixture into a mug.

Makes two servings

INVISIBILITY POTION

1 cup white wine
1 teaspoon poppy seeds

Soak the seeds in the wine for thirteen days, then drink a little of the wine for thirteen days in a row. This creates an aura of invisibility around yourself, so people don't notice you as much.

Makes thirteen daily servings

FAERY GLAMOURY POTION

1 cup boiling water   A pinch of lavender petals
A pinch of rose petals   A pinch of jasmine tea

Put the dry ingredients in a cup. Carefully pour the water into the cup, and let the mixture steep for about 5 minutes. Drink this potion just before you go out on a date or whenever you want to look enchanting.

Makes one cup

WISHING UPON A STAR POTION

1 scoop of vanilla ice cream
½ teaspoon sweetened cocoa
   or chocolate soy drink

¼ cup crushed pecans or
   almonds

Place the scoop of vanilla ice cream in a ceramic or glass bowl, and then using your fingers sprinkle the cocoa in a star shape on the top of the ice cream. Then place a pecan, one at a time, on top of the star shape made in cocoa. All the while you are doing this, focus on your magical wish. Imagine it coming true, right now! As you eat the ice cream, savor the joy of your wish coming true. Feel what it is like to have your wish come true.

Makes one serving

PERSONAL SUCCESS POTION

1 cup apple cider
¼ cup orange juice
1 teaspoon lemon juice
1 teaspoon brown sugar or
   honey

4 whole cloves
1 cinnamon stick broken into
   four pieces

Heat the ingredients in a ceramic pot, but do not boil the mixture. Pour the mixture into a mug, let it cool a bit, and then sip slowly. While you are drinking the potion, visualize your personal success. See and sense your deepest professional goals being attained easily and completely. I suggest you use a lit gold or green candle for focusing while you are sipping the potion.

Makes one serving

PROTECTION OIL POTION

1 pint of extra-light olive oil   1 cup fresh chopped sweet
A dash of lemon juice   basil

Put the lemon juice and basil in a sterile jar, then pour the oil into
the jar. Cover the jar, and refrigerate for ten days. After that time,
take the oil out and leave it at room temperature until it liquifies.
Strain the basil out of the oil. Put the strained oil back into the jar,
cover it, and store the oil in the refrigerator. It will keep for about two
weeks. Use the oil potion in salad dressings, on pasta, potatoes, and on
other foods you eat and cook for those you love. Remember it is
critical that you refrigerate your herb oil potions. The oil will solidify
when chilled, but will become liquid again at room temperature.

Makes one pint

HEALING POTIONS

These potion recipes can be used to promote healing and well-being.

HAPPY POTION

1 cup water
1 teaspoon poppyseeds

Boil the poppyseeds and water in a ceramic pot for 13 minutes. Pour
the brew into a mug and let it cool. Sip the liquid potion, and then
chew the poppyseeds. This potion will relax you and make you feel
happy.

Makes one serving

Tranquility Potion

1 cup boiling water   Honey to taste
1 tablespoon valerian

Put the valerian in a mug, and pour the water over it. Let it steep for
5 minutes. Sweeten the potion with honey to suit your taste. Sip
slowly while listening to soft music or sitting quietly outdoors. This
potion will ease your stress and help you remain calm.

Makes one serving

Isis Healing Potion

1 pint of extra-light olive oil   A pinch of rosemary
1 dry chili pepper   A pinch of sage
A dash of lemon   1 cup fresh chopped tarragon
A pinch of thyme

Put all the ingredients, except the oil, in a sterile jar, then pour the oil
into the jar over the ingredients. Cover the jar and refrigerate for ten
days. After ten days, take the concoction out of the refrigerator and
leave the oil at room temperature until it liquifies, and then strain it.
Put the strained oil back into the jar and cover it, and store the oil in
the refrigerator. It will keep for thirteen days. Use the oil potion in
salad dressings, on fresh and steamed vegetables, potatoes, and toasted
sour dough bread. **Please note:** For safety reasons, you must refrigerate your herb oil potions. Herb oils stored at room temperature
will go bad and can cause botulism! The oil will solidify when
chilled, but will become liquid again at room temperature.

Makes one pint

TAMING THE DRAGON DIET POTION

4 cups boiling water
1 handful roasted barley

Add the roasted barley to a ceramic teapot. Pour the water over the barley and let the mixture steep for 10 minutes. Pour the brew into another pot, straining out the barley, and then chill the potion. Drink 2 cups a day, cold or hot, to help you lose weight.

Makes 4 servings

WARMING POTION

1 cup boiling water
2 teaspoons fresh ginger (you can also use 1 teaspoon of dried powder)

Grate the ginger and then squeeze the juice into a cup of boiling water. Drink the brew immediately. It improves your circulation, helps ease shivering, and warms your body.

Makes one serving

GREEN GODDESS HEALING POTION

3 stalks celery
3 sprigs of parsley
¼ head cabbage

1 clove garlic
1 peeled cucumber
1 cored apple, peeled

All of the ingredients in this potion should be fresh. Juice all the ingredients in a juicer, and then pour the mixture into a glass. For maximum benefit, sip slowly at room temperature.

Makes 1 large serving

AVALON APPLE POTION

2–3 red delicious apples, peeled
2 cups red seedless grapes
6 strawberries

Remove the core and seeds from the apples and then cut them into small pieces that fit easily into your juicer. Remove the tops from the strawberries. Begin by juicing the grapes and strawberries, and then juice the apples. Drink this potion to uplift your spirits and heal your weary mind.

Makes one serving

WAKE UP POTION

A cup boiling water
13 drops fresh lemon or lime juice
1 teaspoon of maple syrup

Pour the lemon juice and maple syrup into the cup of boiling water. Let it cool a little, and then drink this potion first thing in the morning before you eat anything.

Makes one serving

SLEEPING POTION

1 cup water
1 tablespoon sesame seeds

Make this sleeping potion just before you go to bed. Rinse the sesame seeds and put them in a ceramic or glass pot. Then add the water and boil the mixture for 10 minutes. Let the potion cool, and then slowly sip the liquid and chew the seeds.

Makes one serving

SPRING FEVER POTION

5 drops pure vanilla
5 drops lavender essential oil
½ cup warm water

Drop the essential oil and vanilla into a 4 oz. spray bottle filled with warm water. Spray it onto your body, and anything else you want to smell spring fresh!

MAGIC POTION POWDERS

While the powders here won't magically transport you from place to place, they can be used to attract more love, money, and to discover the truth, among other things.

MONEY MAKING POTION

1 pinch oak bark   1 pinch ginger
1 pinch allspice   1 pinch cinnamon
1 pinch orange peel   3 cashews
1 pinch mint

Think of making more money all the while you grind the herbs and the nuts together into a fine powder with your mortar and pestle. Sprinkle a bit of the potion mixture in your wallet, purse, safe, or place of business. Sprinkle the potion on your altar in the shape of a dollar sign, and burn green candles next to the symbol while you focus on attaining your magical goal of creating more prosperity in your life.

SWEET SHEETS POTION

2 pinches rose petals   2 pinches jasmine
2 pinches lavender   2 pinches catnip

Grind the dried herbs together into a fine powder. Focus on bringing more love into your life as you do this. Sprinkle your bed sheets
and bedroom with the powder potion for a sweet evening of love.

ENCHANTED FOREST POTION

1 pinch oak bark   1 pinch lavender
1 pinch pine bark   1 pinch ginger

Grind all of the dried herbs together into a fine powder. As you do
this, imagine yourself in a beautiful enchanted forest. Go deep into
the forest and feel its power and wisdom. Sprinkle tiny bits of the
potion in the four corners of each room in your home, North, East,
South, and West, to create a sanctuary, an enchanted forest.

FORTUNE POTION

1 pinch allspice   1 pinch orange peel
1 pinch nutmeg   1 pinch dill

Grind all of the dried herbs together into a fine powder while focusing on bringing more fortune into your life. Sprinkle the good luck
potion powder around your home, place of business, inside your
shoes, and anywhere you want to be fortunate.

Inside-Outside Protection Potion

1 pinch sea salt   1 pinch cumin
1 pinch mugwort   1 pinch lavender
1 pinch sage   1 clove

Grind all of the dried herbs and salt together into a fine powder. Focus on your magical goal as you do this. Sprinkle the potion powder where you need protection, both indoors and outdoors. You can also sprinkle the powder in a circle to stand in every day until you feel more safe and relaxed.

Truth Potion

1 pinch sage   1 pinch rosemary
1 pinch cedar

Grind all of the dried herbs together into a fine powder. Keep your magical goal in mind while you are doing this. Sprinkle the potion powder in your place of business, in court rooms, or at home.

Country Comfort Potion

A pinch of lavender   A pinch of chamomile
A pinch of sage   A pinch of parsley

All the herbs need to be dried and ground into a powder. Sprinkle the powder around your home, hotel rooms, in your car, your work place, and anywhere you want to feel comfortable or at home.

LUST POTION

1 pinch coriander   1 pinch ginseng
1 pinch jasmine   1 pinch dill

Grind all of the dried herbs together into a fine powder. As you do
this, imagine all of the loving and lustful energies you are imparting
into the mixture. Sprinkle this mixture all over your bedroom.

FERTILITY POTION

1 pinch jasmine   1 pinch oak bark
1 pinch rose petals   1 pinch marjoram

Grind all of the ingredients together into a fine powder. Sprinkle in
your bedroom and under your bed.

POTION INGREDIENTS

The following list will familiarize you with some of ingredients used
in magic potions, along with their magical qualities.

Alfalfa	Prosperity, money, sustenance
Allspice	Money, luck, healing
Almond	Money, prosperity, wisdom
Aloe	Protection, healing, good luck
Apple	Love, happiness, healing, uplifting energy
Apricot	Love, creativity, mental openness
Avocado	Love, beauty, lust
Banana	Fertility, prosperity, potency
Barley	Healing, love, protection, prosperity

Basil	Love, wealth, protection
Bay	Protection, purification, healing, prophecy, enhances psychic powers
Brazil Nut	Romance, love, friendship
Carob	Protection, healing
Carrot	Lust, fertility, healing
Cashew	Money, prosperity
Catnip	Love, lust, joy, beauty, cat magic, relaxes, promotes sleep, happiness
Cedar	Purification, money, protection, healing
Celery	Lust, enhances mental clarity, deepens intuition
Chamomile	Money, love, purification, calming, relaxing
Cherry	Love, divination
Chili pepper	Fidelity, love, passion
Cinnamon	Psychic powers, protection, love power, lust, success, stimulates creativity
Cloves	Protection, prosperity, purification, love, enhances mental powers
Coriander	Love, lust, rejuvenation, passion, strengthens desire
Cucumber	Fertility, healing, lust
Cumin	Protection, fidelity, dispelling negativity
Dill	Protection, money, luck, lust
Garlic	Healing, dispels negativity, wealth, success, good luck
Ginger	Prosperity, love, power, healing, strengthens and warms the spirit
Ginseng	Healing, love, wishes, beauty, protection
Grape	Money, fertility, mental clarity
Honey	Love, prosperity, calms, relaxes and balances
Jasmine	Prosperity, prophetic dreams, lust, passion, love
Lavender	Love, peace, purification, protection, calming, balancing, longevity
Lemon	Purification, love, friendship, clarity, calming, helps mental powers

Lime	Love, protection, healing
Maple	Love, longevity, money
Marjoram	Protection, love, fertility, happiness, prosperity, relaxes nervous tension and exhaustion
Mint	Passion, protection, travel, dispelling negativity, mental clarity, increases memory, enhances concentration
Mugwort	Psychic powers, protection, strength, prophetic dreams, fertility, healing
Nutmeg	Luck, prosperity, fidelity, strengthens, calms, increases dreams
Oak	Money, protection, healing, potency, power, fertility, good luck
Orange	Love, prosperity, divination, luck, relaxing, balancing, stimulating, sensual
Papaya	Love, romance, healing, protection
Parsley	Protection, purification, healing
Peach	Longevity, love, fertility, wishes, dispels negativity
Pecan	Money, good luck, employment
Pine	Fertility, protection, money, healing, dispelling negativity
Poppy seeds	Fertility, love, sleep, money, good luck, invisibility
Raspberry	Protection, love, optimism, brightness, clarity
Rose	Romance, love, luck, divination, protection, peace, balances and strengthens heart chakra
Rosemary	Protection, love, passion, mental powers, purification, uplifting, mental stimulant, strength, courage
Sage	Wisdom, protection, immortality, purification, cleanses, balances and strengthens
Sesame	Prosperity, passion, love, lust, fertility
Strawberry	Love, luck, passion, gifts, joy, happiness, faery magic

Thyme	Healing, sleep, enhances psychic powers, courage, purification, love
Vanilla	Love, lust, passion, mental powers, calms, soothes nerves, relaxes
Valerian	Healing, promotes sleep, calms, soothes emotions, expands awareness, dispels negativity, cat magic

5

MAGIC RITUALS
AND SPELLS

KNOWING WHICH RITUAL and spell to use when the situation calls, is one of the keys to successful magic. Logic, in the sense of knowing how to put a pattern together, is also a necessary part of magic. You must know what practical steps you need to take to attain your magical goals.

Rituals and spells set the stage for empowering your goals. Certain words and rhyming phrases, coupled with the three basic steps of magic (intention and expectation, desire, and merging), can open the right windows and let the magic come into your life. You can use this energy to bring you more love, to create a better relationship, to get a better job, or get better grades in school, among other things.

Successful magic involves setting a pattern in place, and then through spell casting and ritual, building the power of the pattern until it comes to fruition.

Rituals and spells that use incantation and magical focals, such as candles and incense, give sensual form to magical patterns. Through the proper use of magical ingredients, potions, and spells, you give method to your magic. As with all magic, you need to clearly understand the intention, purpose, and ultimate goal of your potion or spell.

Through rituals and spells, you can entice magic to occur in your life. They are ways of communicating with the Divine spirit. Both male and female, this spirit is the infiniteness that connects us all together into one living entity. When you do a ritual and spell, you call upon Divine powers that reach in this Oneness. This Divine connection is the primary key to successful magic making.

DIVINE AND ANCESTRAL HELPERS

Invoking Divine and ancestral energies gives power to your magical patterns. In essence, you are the meeting place between the Divine and your ancestral spirits.

In the mystical traditions, the land is sacred. Our energy, our spirits, are deposited into the land when we die, and then drawn upon at will by succeeding generations. The legend of the sword in the stone and the sorcerer's stone allude to the past and future. By drawing the sword from the stone, you are reclaiming your ancestral heritage. You, and all of us, are descendants of the Divine, no matter what its form.

Essentially magic is an affirmation of the Divine energy within you. All magical energy comes from your connection with the Divine. Rituals and spells reaffirm this connection. A sign that you are doing powerful magic is when after a work, you are filled with an incredible feeling of love that spreads throughout your being like a warm tingling glow.

Go ahead and invoke positive Divine and ancestral energies into your circle when making potions or doing spells. Beware of invoking entities that are obviously dark as they will bring chaos and destruction to your magical patterns. There is "The Threefold Law of Return" that witches and wizards follow. It states that any negative magic you do will come back to you three times as strong. So do only good works, and stay away from the dark side, or it will seek to destroy you.

By using helpful entities, you bring their energy to life. Which Divine energies you ask to help you depends on the potion you are making and the spell you are doing. For example, in a love spell, you could ask love goddesses such as Aphrodite, Freya, or Venus to guide you and bless your spell.

Before beginning a particular ritual or spell, first read it over so you know what ingredients you will need to gather together prior to doing it. Make sure you have everything you will need, including matches, because once you begin casting a spell, you don't want to have to interrupt the flow. You are creating energetic patterns, and once a magical pattern begins, a flow or momentum is created that can be amplified for maximum success.

Nine-Point Spell Checklist

1. Write down the kind of spell you are doing and for what purpose into your book of shadows or in a magic journal. Write down what your intentions and expectations are for the spell or ritual.
2. Write down the date, day of the week, and time you cast the spell.
3. Write down any significant corresponding astrological information such as sun sign, moon phase, and so forth.
4. Gather together all of the items you will need, and set up your altar.
5. Prepare your magical space.
6. Invite helpful Divine energies, Goddesses, Gods, power animals, elementals, guides, and other allies into your circle.
7. Cast the spell. Keep this book handy while you are working.
8. Write down the results of your efforts. Remember with some spells and rituals, it may be necessary to wait awhile to enter this information.
9. Write down any additional comments, suggestions, or personal observations.

A Grimoire of Magic Spells

Each spell and ritual has a listing of ingredients needed as well as easy-to-follow instructions. When starting out, follow the rituals and spells as they are written. Once you become familiar with them, feel free to adapt them to better fit your situation. You can always change the words and ingredients to fit your needs. The idea is to have fun while attaining your magical goals. Also, feel free to add some of the magic potions you make to the spells. For example, you could add the True Love Potion to the High Moon Love Spell. Adding potions that you make to spells doubles their magical power!

LOVE SPELLS

FRIENDSHIP OIL SPELL

A pink candle
A vial of strawberry oil

A tiny quartz crystal (small enough to fit into the vial)

CASTING THE SPELL
Draw a magic circle and call in the elemental powers. Light the candle, and invite your favorite God or Goddess into the circle. Hold the vial of oil in your hands, rolling it between them so that it becomes warm. Add the tiny crystal to the bottle of oil. Then roll the oil in between your hands again, and say,

> *Oil of friendship, caring, sharing, and beauty*
> *Bring the joy and happiness of friendship to me*
> *By the power of the element, as I will, so shall it be!*

Place the vial of oil on your altar for thirteen days. After this time, use the friendship oil for anointing yourself just prior to going out to parties, class, sporting events, work, or whenever you want to make new friends.

GYPSY MOON LOVE SPELL

A 7-inch blade of grass, oatstraw, or other edible grass

CASTING THE SPELL

Cut a 7-inch blade of grass at midnight on a full moon. Before the clock strikes 1:00 A.M., hold the blade of grass in your mouth, face East, and say,

> *Before the next rising sun*
> *(Insert name) shall hear my call*
> *Before the sun shall set*
> *(Insert name) for me shall fall.*

Face West, and repeat,

> *Before the next rising sun*
> *(Insert name) shall hear my call*
> *Before the sun shall set*
> *(Insert name) for me shall fall.*

Then cut the blade of grass into minuscule pieces. Invite the one you are trying to attract to lunch or dinner, and mix the tiny grass pieces with his or her food, and he or she will fall passionately and completely in love with you.

RED ROSE LOVE RITUAL

A chalice filled with grape juice

A red rose or dried red rose petals

A red candle

A ballpoint pen or quill

Rose oil

CASTING THE SPELL

Do this spell just before you go to sleep. Wash the candle in cool water, dry it, and then place it on your altar. Next, draw a magic circle and call in the elemental powers. Use the rose oil to anoint your forehead, both wrists, and ankles. Now use the ballpoint pen to write the words "*love*" and "*joy*" on the candle body. Next rub a thin coat of rose oil on the candle, and put it back in its holder. Light the candle, merge with the powers of Fire, and say,

> *This flame ignites the passion,*
> *Bring my true love to me,*
> *In a heat that lasts forever.*
> *So be it! So shall it be!*

Hold the chalice of juice in your hands and say,

> *Bring my true love to me,*
> *My sweet love to be.*
> *I offer to you this toast,*
> *So that our love will flow!*

Take the rose (or dried petals), and holding it in your hands, say,

> *My true love, I call to you,*
> *On a bed of roses, pink and blue.*
> *A thousand fragrant flowers,*
> *For us to wile away the hours.*
> *If these pleasures, you desire,*
> *Come be my love, in passion's fire.*
> *So be it! So shall it be!*

Then take the petals off the rose, one at a time, and place a few on your pillow and a couple on the floor by your bed. Snuff the candle out with your wet fingers or a snuffer. A seashell works great for this purpose. As you drift to sleep, imagine your true love coming into your life. Repeat to yourself, "True love come to me." In the morning, light the candle again, and let it burn all the way down. Then, release the elements and pull up the circle. Scatter the rose petals outside your front door to attract your true love.

HIGH MOON LOVE SPELL

A white candle

Sandalwood incense and
   censor

A ballpoint pen or quill

A silver needle or pin

A photo of your lover or
   prospective lover

Soft music

CASTING THE SPELL

Do this spell on a full moon. Set up your altar, and then draw a magic circle of light and call in the elemental powers. Invite your favorite love goddess or god into the circle, and then light the incense and turn on some soft music. Inscribe your initials and your lover's initials in the candle. Do this so the initials overlap each other. Place the photo in front of the candle. Take the silver needle and bathe it in the incense smoke for a few moments, and then pierce the wick of the unlit candle with it. Leave the needle in the candle wick. Light the candle, merge with the passionate power of Fire, and say,

> *Sacred flame of the full moon,*
> *Fill me with love and make it soon.*
> *Sacred light, burn bright,*
> *Bring to me my soul's delight.*
> *Blessed be! So mote it be!*

Gaze into the candle as the candle burns down. As you do this, imagine being with your love. Take the silver needle and fasten it to the right top corner of the photo. Place the photo with the needle under your bed. Lastly, bid farewell to the elements, thank deity, and pull up the circle.

HAPPY FAMILY RITUAL

A white candle
Lavender incense and censor
A chalice or cup filled with
   water

6 pinches crushed rosemary,
   in a bowl

CASTING THE SPELL

Set up your altar, put the rosemary in the bowl, and draw a magic circle. As you do this, imagine the circle surrounding your entire home. Light the candle and incense, and invite your favorite Divine energies into the circle.

Carefully take the burning incense from the altar, and hold it in your hands. Face East, and wave the incense three times, side-to-side. Merge with the powers of Air, and say,

> *Powers of the East, masters of air*
> *I greet, honor, and welcome you here!*
> *Powers of the East, masters of the four winds*
> *Bring happiness to my family and be my friend!*

Set the incense down on the altar, and hold the lit candle. Face South, and wave the candle from side-to-side three times, being careful of dripping wax. Merge with the powers of Fire, and say,

> *Powers of the South, masters of fire*
> *I greet, honor, and welcome you here!*
> *Powers of the South, masters of light*
> *Bring happiness to my family and blessings bright!*

Set the candle on the altar, and hold the chalice in your hands. Face West, dip your fingers into the water, and sprinkle the West point. Do this three times, while merging with the powers of Water, and say,

> *Powers of the West, masters of water*
> *I greet, honor, and welcome you here!*

Powers of the West, masters of fin and fish
Bring happiness to my family and grant my wish!

Set the chalice on the altar, and take the bowl of rosemary in your hands. Face North, and sprinkle three pinches of the herb onto the floor. Merge with the powers of Earth, and say,

Powers of the North, masters of Earth
I greet, honor, and welcome you here!
Powers of the North, masters of the sacred land
Bring happiness to my family and lend a helping hand!

Place the bowl back on the altar. Facing your altar, raise your arms upward. Merge with Oneness, and say,

Helpful powers of Earth, Air, Fire, and Water
I greet, honor, and welcome you here!
Bring happiness to my family
So be it! Blessed be!

Take the bowl of rosemary and scatter tiny bits throughout the corners of your home. Start just inside your front door, and move clockwise. Cover the four corners of each room with a tiny sprinkle. When you are done, gaze at the candle flame on the altar for a few minutes. Imagine the candle flame being a bright spirit light. Close your eyes, and begin to see and feel the white spirit light growing larger and filling yourself, your bedroom, and your entire home with happy, joyful, and loving energy. Allow the candle to burn down completely. Then bid farewell to the elements, thank deity, and pull up the circle. Pour the altar water into a favorite house plant.

MAGIC FRIEND SPELL

Fresh flowers   Vanilla oil
A white candle   A small white stone
A ballpoint pen

CASTING THE SPELL

Set the fresh flowers on your altar. Then wash the candle in cool water, dry it, and place it on the altar. Next, draw a magic circle and call in the elemental powers. Invoke your favorite goddess or god by chanting their names three times. Use the pen to write the words "Magic Friend" on the candle body, and then rub the candle with a thin film of vanilla oil. When you are done, put the candle in its holder on the altar. Next, anoint yourself with the vanilla oil, rubbing three drops on both of your feet, knees, hips, elbows, and hands, along with three drops on your forehead, finishing with three drops on the top of your head. You will smell yummy, just like a chocolate chip cookie! Next, apply three drops of oil to the stone. Hold the stone in your receiving hand, and say,

> *Powers of Earth, powers divine*
> *Our energies do entwine*
> *Bring my magic friend to me*
> *So be it! Blessed be!*

Continue holding the stone, and begin imagining your magic friend, with all of the qualities you admire. See and sense yourself reaching out and really getting in touch with this magic friend. Feel the joy and wonder of your friendship and connection. After doing this for a few minutes, put the stone back upon the altar, and wipe the oil from your hands. Then light the candle, merge with the flame, and say,

> *Candle, candle, light the way*
> *Candle, candle, that I may*
> *See my magic friend in your light*
> *Bless me now, and give me sight.*

Continue gazing at the candle, noticing it is a beacon of magic light, a beacon that draws your magic friend closer. Keep gazing at the flame while you call out the qualities that you desire in a magic friend, such as loyalty, honesty, and humor, as well as kindness, a helping hand, trust, and creativity. Call to your magic friend. Do this out loud in a strong determined voice. Explain that your friendship is a two-way exchange, and that they, too, will benefit from your connection. State what you are willing to give, and what you want to receive from the magic friendship. Be specific. Ask your friend to help you attain your magical goals.

After you are finished calling out to your magic friend, imagine his or her face in the candle flame. Do this for a few minutes. Sit back, holding the stone in your hand, and send your magic friend a special message, or ask a pressing question. Make a mental note of your experience. When you are finished, bid farewell to the elements, thank your magic friend, and pull up the circle. Use the stone anytime you want to communicate with your magic friend.

PROSPERITY SPELLS

PROSPERITY QUICKSPELL

Sage and cedar smudge   A green doormat
A silver coin

CASTING THE SPELL

This is a quick and easy spell designed to bring great riches to your doorstep. First light the smudge, and carefully pass the coin through the smoke to clear it of any unwanted energies. Also pass the doormat through the smoke, and then put the doormat in front of the main entrance door of your home. Next, hold the coin between your hands, and say,

> *North, East, South, and West*
> *By the Lady, I am divinely blessed*
> *Bring great riches to my doorstep*
> *From the North, East, South, and West*
> *As I will, so shall it be!*

Now put the coin under the doormat, and leave it there, to attract money and prosperity. Recharge the coin every month to bring more riches into your life.

APPLE TREE WEALTH SPELL

3 slices of bread
A cup of apple cider

CASTING THE SPELL
You will need to locate a fruiting apple tree to do this spell. Place the slices of bread on the tree branches and pour the cider onto the roots. As you do this say,

> *Blessed be, fruiting apple tree*
> *Now bring great wealth to me*
> *Hats full! Pockets full!*
> *Bushel by bushel-sacks full!*
> *Thank you, great apple tree*
> *Blessed be! So shall it be!*

As the apples grow and ripen, so will your wealth.

SUDDEN SUCCESS SPELL

A green candle
Sandalwood incense and
  censor
A pinch of cinnamon

A pinch of dried rosemary
A piece of orange peel
A green sock or pouch

CASTING THE SPELL
Draw a magic circle, call in the elemental powers, and invite your favorite Divine energies into your circle. Light the candle and incense. Bathe the sock in the incense smoke for a couple of minutes.

Then open it up, and place inside the sock the pinch of rosemary, the pinch of cinnamon, and the piece of orange peel. Then tie the sock closed. To empower your charm, hold it in your hands, and say three times,

> *Sudden success come to me and grow,*
> *Sudden success come to me and flow.*
> *By the elemental powers, now make it so!*

As the candle burns down, imagine experiencing sudden and lasting success, for example, at school, at work, or in your love life. Let your imagination run wild! Let the candle burn down all the way as you do this. Bid farewell to the elements, thank deity, and pull up the circle. Keep the sock or pouch at work, in your desk drawer, or by your computer, to attract sudden success.

THREE WISHES SPELL

Favorite music   3 walnuts
3 green candles   A wand
A ballpoint pen

CASTING THE SPELL

Put on your favorite music. Next, draw a triple magic circle of green light and call in the elemental powers. Use the pen to write your three wishes on the candle bodies, one wish per candle, using as few words as possible. Place the candles, side-by-side, in their holders upon the altar. Then put a walnut next to each of the three candles. Light the candles, one at a time, from left to right, and as you do, state the wish the candle represents. After you are finished lighting the candles and stating your wishes aloud, tap the left-most walnut three times with your wand, and say,

Grant me my wish
It is (re-state the wish that corresponds to that candle)
So be it! So shall it be!
Blessed be, Blessed be, Blessed be!

Do this with each of the three walnuts, until you have re-stated all three of your wishes. Allow the candles to burn down completely, and as you meditate on the flames, say, "My three wishes are coming true, right now."

See and sense your wishes as if they have already come true. Feel the sensations of happiness and joy. When you are done, bid farewell to the elements, thank deity, and pull up the circle. Leave the walnuts on your altar. Crack and eat them as your three wishes come true.

FULL MOON MONEY SPELL

A silver pillar candle   Almond oil
A pinch of allspice

CASTING THE SPELL

On a waxing moon, set up your altar, cast a magic circle, and call in the elemental powers. Inscribe the candle with the exact amount of money you need. Next, dress the candle with almond oil. As you do this, chant over and over,

As the moon waxes and grows
So to me does money flow.

Once the candle is charged with your desire, roll it in the allspice. Put it in a candle holder on your altar and light it. Let the candle burn for an hour, and then snuff it out with your wet fingers. Repeat this spell every night, at the same time, until the moon is completely full. Let the candle burn all the way down on the full moon. The money you desire should come to you by the next full moon.

BANK ON IT MONEY SPELL

2 green candles	Amber scented oil
A green stone	

CASTING THE SPELL

Draw a magic circle of white light, and then draw another circle of green light on top of the first circle. Call in the elemental powers. Next, light the candles, dedicating them to your favorite goddess and god of prosperity, such as Boann and Dagda (Celtic) or Juno and Jupiter (Roman). Hold the stone in your hands and put three drops of scented oil on it. Rub the oil into the stone, and then put it in front of the candles where you can easily see it. Anoint yourself with the oil.

Merge with the Divine and fill your mind with a bright green light, the color of money. Imagine an intense flow of green light, of money and prosperity coming into your life, and allow those images and sensations to fill your mind. Now, it's as if you are going to actually plant your money and prosperity thought-energy into the stone. Do this by imagining a bright beam of green light moving from your forehead and your hands into the stone. Direct your feelings and every ounce of your attention into the stone. Actually allow yourself to see and sense your prosperity thought-energy and feelings being absorbed into the atomic structure of the stone. Then empower your stone by holding it in your hands, and repeating these words three times,

Bring me money, and bring it fast
Grant me prosperity, and make it last

By the powers of Earth, Air, Fire, and Sea
As I will, so shall it be!

Hold the stone and imagine a bright field of green energy surrounding the stone, and shooting out ten feet in all directions from it. See and sense the money stone's field of influence a total of three times to set it in place.

When you have completed these steps, put the stone on your altar for a moment, and clap your hands together three times. Allow the candles to burn down completely, and as you gaze at their light, hold your money talisman in your receiving hand. When you are finished, release the elements, thank deity, and pull up the circle. Carry your talisman in your purse or pants pocket, and enjoy the money that flows into your bank account.

Lucky Coins and Leprechauns Spell

Two green candles   Sandalwood incense and censor
A silver dollar   Bowl of water

Casting the Spell
Do this money spell whenever you see a rainbow. Draw a magic circle and call in the elements. Put the bowl of water in the center of your altar. Put one candle in front of the bowl, and the other one behind it. Light the incense and candles on your altar, and dedicate them to a favorite goddess or god. Invite deity into the circle and ask for blessing and guidance. Bathe the silver dollar in the incense smoke for a minute. Then hold the coin in your hands, and say,

Magic leprechauns, please bless this coin
Bring me treasure and bring it soon

Bring me a rainbow of fortune
By the powers of Earth, Air, Fire, and Sea
As I will, so shall it be! Blessed be!

Now put the coin in the bowl of water. Gaze into the water, watching the reflection of the candles dance on its surface. Imagine your luck and wealth growing. Enjoy the feeling of being so incredibly fortunate. Do this as you watch the candles burn down. Then bid farewell to the elements, thank deity, and pull up the circle. Put the silver dollar into your pocket, wallet, or purse. Pour the water into a favorite houseplant or just outside your front door to attract more luck and wealth.

THREE CANDLE MONEY SPELL

| 3 white candles | Cinnamon oil |
| A ballpoint pen | Salt water |

CASTING THE SPELL

Wash the candles in cool salt water, dry them, and put them on the altar. Draw a triple circle of white light, and then call in the elemental powers. Use the pen to inscribe the amount of money you want on each of the candles. Dress the candles by rubbing them with the oil. Put them side-by-side on the altar. Wipe your hands, and then light the middle candle. Use it to light the other two. As you light each of the candles, merge with the powers of Fire, and say,

As I light this candle,
I see (state the amount of money you want) coming my way
I know my magical goal is coming true.

Gaze into the candle light, and merge with the Fire spirit. Take a few deep breaths, and merge a little deeper with the flames. Imagine the amount of money you want in the flame. See the symbol and numbers, see gold or cash. Do this for several minutes. Close your eyes, and see and sense your magical goal coming true in the near future. Take your time. When you are finished, open your eyes, gaze at the candles, and say,

> *I see (state the amount of money you want) coming my way*
> *I know my magical goal is coming true.*
> *As I will, so be it! Blessed be!*

Allow the candles to safely burn down on their own, and then bid farewell to the elements, thank deity, and pull up the circle.

You can repeat this spell as often as you like.

EMPOWERMENT SPELLS

NON-MAGICALS ENLIGHTENMENT SPELL

A white candle
A chalice of water

A white altar cloth
Paper and pen

CASTING THE SPELL:

Cover your altar with the white altar cloth, and then put the candle in a holder and the chalice of water on it. Draw a magic circle, set the elemental powers in place, and invite your favorite Divine energies into the circle. As you light the candle, imagine your life being filled with like-minded people; those that believe in magic. As you light the candle say three times,

> *Candle of magic, white candle light*
> *Enlighten all non-magicals, make them bright!*

Hold the chalice of water upward in your hands, merge with the
power of Water, and empower the liquid by saying,

> *As the tides flow and the moon spins,*
> *May the non-magicals be enlightened, and the magic begin*
> *May we merry meet and blessed be,*
> *So be it! So mote it be!*

Swirl the water around clockwise in the chalice three times. Do this
carefully so that none of it splashes out. As you do this, imagine the
water being filled with Divine energy. Then drink the water from the
chalice. Sit or recline comfortably in front of your altar, and start to
think of steps you can personally take to bring more magic into your
life and into the lives of those you love. Make some brief notes to
refer to later. Use the candle light as a meditative tool, merging with
the powers of fire. When you are finished, bid farewell to the elements, thank the Divine energies that helped you, and pull up the
circle. In the next few days, refer to your notes and take some of the
steps you wrote down.

TREE WISHING SPELL

A living tree	A small piece of paper
A yellow ribbon	A green felt pen

CASTING THE SPELL

Use the green felt pen to write your wish on the piece of paper. Roll
the paper into a scroll, and then tie it with the ribbon into the tree. Say,

> *Joy be free, joy be free*
> *By rain and winds come loose*
> *May my wish come to me.*
> *Blessed be! So mote it be!*

With the wind and rain, your wish is liberated from the tree and it is free to come true.

SUNFLOWER POWER SPELL

A package of sunflower seeds
A gold candle

CASTING THE SPELL

Draw a magic circle of golden light, and then call in the elemental powers. Light the candle, dedicating it to a goddess of abundance such as Fortuna. Put the seed packet in front of the candle, and imagine planting the sunflowers in the package. See your self watering and cultivating them. In your mind's eye, watch the flowers grow big and tall. Now pick up the seed packet and empower it by saying,

Sunflower seeds, bring me power
Growing stronger with each passing hour
Bring great success and let it grow
As I will, it shall be so!

Hold the seeds in your hands until the packet feels warm to the touch. Put the packet back upon your altar in front of the candle. Imagine the sunflowers blooming and thriving, and begin to chant,

Sunflowers bring me power.
Let it grow, let it grow.

Let the candle burn down on its own. Bid farewell to the elements, thank deity, and pull up the circle. Take the seed packet and plant the seeds in a sunny location, thanking the elemental powers of Earth, Air, Fire, Water, and spirit as you do so. Water them regularly and watch them grow. As they grow stronger, your power also grows stronger.

DO YOU BELIEVE IN MAGIC RITUAL

3 white candles	A silver bell
Lavender scented oil	

CASTING THE SPELL

Wash the candles in cool water, dry them, and then rub lavender oil on them. Put them in their holders on the altar. Anoint yourself with the lavender oil. Then draw a magic circle of bright green light and call in the elemental powers. Ring the bell three times each time you light one of candles. When all of the candles are lit, say,

> *Magic rings, three times three*
> *Spells and dreams, red and green*
> *By the powers of Earth, Air, Fire, and Sea*
> *By the ancient powers of the faeries*
> *Bless my life with magic. Blessed be!*

Now ring the bell seven times, and then sit back. Breathe rhythmically to the count of three: breathe in, counting to three, hold your breath for three counts, then exhale to the count of three. Do this three times. Then begin to imagine yourself standing in the middle of a circular grove of oak trees. Walk over to the oak closest to you, and touch the coarseness of the oak tree's bark. The moment your skin makes contact with the tree, you see a circular chasm abruptly appear in the ground at the foot of the oak. It looks like a dark green ring, a magical ring that opens into a different reality—an Otherworld. As you look deep into the opening, you can see strange yet familiar people in this place, fertile fields, gleaming rivers twisting to the seas, as well as forests and dwellings.

You enter the opening, climbing through the ring and down into the chasm, following a long steep winding passageway. Moving to the end of the passageway, you find yourself at the edge of a bright, moonlit village. An oddly refreshing wind flips across the land and over your skin, and suddenly everything seems filled with the curious stillness of a magical realm. You begin to see and sense the starspun faeries gathering all around you, communicating with you. You can see and sense their energies empowering you, and filling you with brilliant starlight. Allow the starspun faery light to completely fill you. Write down your experience in your book of shadows if you like.

Allow the candles to safely burn down on their own, and then ring the bell three times. Thank the faeries, bid farewell to the elements, and pull up the circle. Put a few drops of the lavender oil on a cotton ball or handkerchief, and put it in your pocket or desk. Take it out to remind you that the world is a magical place.

MAKING THE BEST CHOICE SPELL

A stone   A ballpoint pen
A yellow candle   Clary sage oil

CASTING THE SPELL

Do this spell just before you go to sleep. Wash the candle in cool water, dry it, and use the pen to write the words "best choice" on it. Dress the candle with the oil and anoint the stone. Then anoint yourself by putting a drop on your forehead, and a couple of drops on your wrists and ankles. While you are doing this, think about the choice you need to make. Examine all sides of the choice. Then draw a magic circle and call in the elements. Ask deity into your circle. Light the candle, merge with the powers of Fire, and say,

> *As I dream I will know*
> *The best choice to make*
> *When I wake, I will remember*
> *The best choice to make*
> *So be it! Blessed be!*

Focus on the flame of the candle for a few minutes. Either snuff out the candle, or allow it to burn out on its own in a fireproof container. Lie back in bed, holding the stone in your receiving hand. Close your eyes, and as you drift to sleep, repeat,

> *When I wake, I remember*
> *The best choice to make.*

Upon waking, rub the stone in your hand, and try to recall everything you can about your dream. Write down any decision you came to in your dream. Think about your choice again, and check out how you feel about it. When you are done, thank deity, release the elements, and pull up the magic circle. Repeat this spell until you know the right choice to make.

DIETING DRAGON DREAM SPELL

Cedar incense and censer   Dragon's blood oil
A white candle   A feather
A ballpoint pen   Salt water

CASTING THE SPELL

Wash the candle in cool salt water, dry it, and then place it on the altar. Draw a magic circle and call in the elemental powers. Next, light the incense, and then use the pen to write the words "Tame the Dragon," on the candle body. Carve your initials on top of the words, and then dress the candle with the dragon's blood oil. Put the candle in its holder on the altar. Wipe the oil off your hands, and light the candle. As you do, merge with the salamander spirit (a small dragon) within the candle, and say,

> *Dragon spirit of Fire and candle light*
> *Help me tame the dieting dragon tonight.*
> *As I will, so mote it be!*

Next, bathe the feather in the smoke for a few minutes, hold it in your dominant hand, and say,

> *Smoke of the dragon*
> *Transform my body,*
> *Light as a feather*
> *Shedding my unwanted weight,*
> *Eating foods that are healthy*
> *Fresh and alive with energy,*
> *With this, I can be the shape I want to be.*
> *So be it! So dream it!*

Place the feather on your altar in front of the candle. Let the candle burn down on its own, and as you drift to sleep, imagine yourself being light as a feather.

In the morning, pull up the magic circle, thank the dragon spirits, and bid farewell to the elements. Stick the feather on your refrigerator as a reminder that you have successfully tamed the dragon, and are on your way to losing that unwanted weight and becoming light as a feather.

BELLE OF THE BALL BEAUTY SPELL

A silver bell
A fancy handkerchief
A small handheld mirror

A pair of comfortable,
nice-looking shoes

CASTING THE SPELL

Like the Faery Godmother in the story of "Cinderella," the sound of the bell can transform you into the "belle of the ball." The word belle means "beautiful." The best time to do this spell is on a clear night when the moon is bright.

Put on the pair of shoes. Gather together all the items and take everything outdoors. Be sure to cast this spell somewhere private where you won't be disturbed. Draw a magic circle of bright white light around the area in which you will be working. Next, face the full moon, and ring the bell nine times. Spread the handkerchief on the ground in front of you, and put the bell on top of it. Gaze at the moon for a few minutes, merging with its bright light. Then, invoke the goddess in her lunar aspect by saying,

> Great Goddess-Mother of lunar light,
> Queen of the sky and seas.
> Great Lady of the starry night,
> Goddess Mother of the ancient mysteries,
> Hear the bell as it rings out to you,
> Bless me with your beauty through and through.

Hold the mirror facing the full moon, so it reflects the moon's light. Keeping the mirror angled toward the moon, take three steps slowly around the silver bell in a clockwise circle. As you do this, watch the reflected moonlight in the mirror shooting out over the area around you as you move. Keep moving in a clockwise circle, gradually increasing your speed, all the while watching as the moonlight fills the mirror and dances over your surroundings. Now angle the mirror so the reflected light of silvery moon spreads over your face, body, and shoes. Breathe deeply a few times, and inhale the power of the beautiful, bright moonlight. Fill yourself to the brim with this lunar energy, and then run clockwise around the circle three times, chanting these words,

> Silver ball of the moon,
> By bell, mirror, and shoes,
> May my beauty bloom!
> As I will, make it so!

Pick up the bell, and ring it three times. Give thanks to the moon goddess, bid farewell to the elemental powers, and pull up the circle. Bring everything back indoors. Carry the handkerchief in your purse or pocket, and wear the shoes when you to want to look and feel more beautiful.

SPIRIT GUIDE RITUAL

Sandalwood incense   A wand
Lavender oil

CASTING THE SPELL

Use this spell whenever you need a little Divine guidance. Draw a magic circle and call in the elemental powers. Then light the incense, dedicating it to your favorite Divine energies. Use the base of your wand to knock nine times in the middle of the altar. Put your wand back upon the altar. Anoint yourself with the oil, applying three drops to your third eye (on your forehead, in between your eyebrows), three drops to your throat, and three drops to the insides of both your wrists and ankles. Hold your wand in your hands and say,

> *Spirit guide, guiding light*
> *Visit with me on this starry night.*
> *Magic friend, so true and bright*
> *Show yourself to me tonight.*

Continue holding your wand and begin to imagine a glowing silver-white light flowing and swirling around you, wrapping you in its beauty. Feel the energy of the silver-white light filling you with its power. Now imagine yourself standing in a sunny green meadow. You notice a stone pathway on the far end of the meadow. The path is practically hidden by flowers spilling over it, and there are large apple trees, heavy with ripe golden fruit, shading the pathway. You follow the path under an archway made of yellow climbing roses, and enter a magical garden filled with roses of every color and fragrant clumps of thick lavender. A wisteria vine with smooth skin is covered with dense fragrant purple flowers. The scents from the flowers completely fill your senses, and you breathe in the beauty of the garden.

As you enjoy the wonders of the magical garden, you begin to notice that you are not alone. You look around you and see an image of your spirit guide nearby. You invite him or her to come closer. Greet your spirit guide, and ask his or her name. Address your spirit guide by name, and then ask a pressing question that has been on your mind. You can do this aloud or silently. Spend some time communicating with him or her, and then thank your spirit guide.

Use your wand to knock three times when you are done, and then come back to the present time and place. Thank your spirit guide, the Divine energies that helped you with your spell, and then bid farewell to the elemental powers. Pull up your circle. Whenever you want to communicate with your spirit guide, just sit quietly, hold your wand in your hands, and imagine yourself being in the magical garden with your spirit guide.

THE CRYSTAL DOOR RITUAL

A quartz crystal
A white candle
Frankincense and myrrh
   incense and censor

A bowl of salt
A chalice of water
Soft music

CASTING THE SPELL

Put on some soft music, draw a magic circle, and call in the elemental powers. Next, light the candle and incense. To cleanse the crystal of unwanted energies, put it in the bowl of salt and roll it around, saying,

Begone all evil and foulness
Begone from this stone now and forevermore!

Next, hold the crystal in your power hand. Merge with the crystal—
the Earth element—and say,

> *I empower this crystal with the powers of Earth.*
> *So be it! As I will, so shall it be!*

Still holding the crystal in your power hand, bathe it in the incense
smoke for a few minutes. Merge with the Air element, and say,

> *I empower this crystal with the powers of Air.*
> *So be it! As I will, so shall it be!*

Now move the crystal carefully around the flame of the candle in a
clockwise circle, at a safe distance. Merge with the Fire element, and say,

> *I empower this crystal with the powers of Fire.*
> *So be it! As I will, so shall it be!*

Next, sprinkle nine drops of water on the crystal. Merge with the
powers of Water, and say,

> *I empower this crystal with the powers of Water.*
> *So be it! As I will, so shall it be!*

Then hold the stone in both of your hands, and say,

> *I empower this crystal with helpful powers*
> *Of Earth, Air, Fire, and Water*
> *So be it! As I will, so shall it be!*

Next, sit or recline comfortably, holding your crystal in your hands,
and close your eyes. Take a few deep breaths, and let go of any tensions or worries for a little while. Begin imagining yourself walking
down a path through a wooded forest in the afternoon. There are
oak, pine, madrone, and fir trees all around you, and you can smell the
scent of the trees in the air. Deer appear now and again, and you can
hear the birds singing.

As you walk down the path, you come to a magnificent tree made
of brilliant crystal. You move closer to the stone tree, feeling the

smooth crystal trunk beneath your hands. The stone feels amazingly warm to your touch. You gently pat the stone tree trunk nine times with your right hand; one-two-three, one-two-three, one-two-three. As you do this, the tree trunk opens up to reveal a hidden doorway.

The hush of the forest around you becomes pronounced, and you feel a blast of hot air, and suddenly find yourself in a dim underground chamber with black and gray walls. You notice that the darkened chamber opens up into a large, brighter chamber. You enter the second chamber and see that you have entered a cave. The walls around you are covered with dark red garnets and purple-red rubies. You can feel the power from the red stone walls flowing into you, and you take a deep breath and fill your being with the refreshing, red glowing energy. As you walk further into the cave, the garnets and rubies change to softly glowing orange carnelian. You take another deep breath, filling your being with the orange glowing energy. As you move even further into the cave, the orange glowing walls become golden, made of citrine and golden topaz. You take a deep breath, filling your being with the golden light around you. As you take a few more steps, you notice the walls are now covered with green malachite, and then the malachite changes into walls made of bright green emeralds. You can feel the balancing energy radiating from the emerald walls, and you take a deep breath, absorbing all of the emerald energy. The green walls become turquoise blue, and then deep blue sapphire. You breathe in their energy, and then take a few more steps into the cave. Suddenly you find yourself completely surrounded by purple amethyst. You slowly absorb the power of the amethyst. Now allow the power and knowledge of the crystal cave to fill you to the brim. Drink in the Divine energy of the magical cave.

When you are finished, thank the crystal spirits, and then move your awareness back to the present time and place. Allow the candle to safely burn down on its own. Release the elements, thank deity, and pull up the circle. Keep the crystal on your altar to use whenever you want to return to the crystal cave. For more information on the magical uses of crystals, please refer to my book, *The Pocket Guide to Crystals and Gemstones* (Crossing Press, 1998).

Favorite Pet Protection Spell

A full moon
Venus water (Refer to the recipe for Venus water in chapter 4, p. 67.)
Your pet

Casting the Spell
Sit or recline with your pet outside under the moon, or indoors where you can see the moon. Talk with your pet, and praise him or her. Tell your animal friend how much you care for him or her. Most of us have little nicknames and words of endearment we say to our pets. As you do this, imagine a protective sphere of bright white light surrounding your pet. Next, take the Venus water, and anoint your pet with three drops, stroking the water into the animal's fur or skin. As you do this, merge with your pet, and say this protective blessing,

> I call upon the Moon Goddess and Horned God,
> I call upon the starspun powers of Oneness,
> I call upon all of the living creatures of the earth
> By Earth, Air, Fire, and Water, by Divine will,
> I ask that you work this protective spell,
> Please guard (insert name of pet) while sleeping and waking,
> And protect this animal from all negativity and harm.
> In all worlds, in all times! So be it! Blessed be!

Tell your pet how much you love him or her, and then let your pet go. Clap your hands three times. I also suggest using brown or blue dog collars for your pet, with a hematite ring and a tag of identification securely fastened to the collar. I haven't had much luck using collars with my cats. They always manage to pull them off. Every day, to reinforce the protective energy of this spell, take a few minutes and imagine your pet being surrounded with a protective sphere of divine white light.

MAKING A MAGIC POOKA

A white candle

A place for your pooka to live (a ring, pendant, stone, or coin)

A sheet of paper

A pen

A large mirror

CASTING THE SPELL

The pooka in Irish legends was often a shape shifter who could appear in human or animal form. Similar to the brownie, pookas are energetic beings who are friendly, helpful, and well-disposed to mortals.

Before beginning, decide what you intend to create, and where you are going to house your pooka. Rings, pendants, stones, or coins all make good homes. Avoid using electronic devices because their magnetic fields can be disrupted by this process. Also situate yourself in such a way so you can look into a large mirror while you do this work. Then read over the following steps a few times before attempting them.

1. Determine your pooka's nature. Imagine it in your mind. For example, does it look like a cat, owl, wolf, horse, or large white rabbit?

2. Determine how long it will live. Will it be a lifelong companion? If so, select a word or simple phrase that will free it at the time of your death, so it can live on.

3. Decide what tasks it will perform. Do you want it to protect you, bring more love and prosperity into your life, help you attain your magical goals, inspire your creativity, or all of the above?

4. Determine its food supply and basis of nourishment. For example, it can live off of sound, hydrogen, or light.

5. Decide upon your pooka's name so you can easily summon it.

6. Write down all of these details (1–5) on a sheet of paper.

7. Draw a magic circle, and set the elemental powers in place. Light the candle, and begin staring into the mirror. You should be able to see the reflection of both of your hands clearly in the looking glass. If not, re-position the mirror and yourself so that you can see your hands clearly.

8. Next, merge with the intention and expectation of successfully creating your pooka. Focus all of your attention on the task. Your pooka's abilities and level of power correspond directly to the depth of your merge. As you merge deeply, and then deeper still, watch your reflection in the mirror, and begin imagining yourself actually holding a sphere or ball of pure light. Continue watching your reflection in the mirror, and then begin to shape this bright ball of energy with your mind and hands, molding the energy with your intention and kneading it with your hands, creating your pooka exactly as you imagined it. Make it so that there is no distinction between you and your image in the mirror.

9. Then place your pooka in its home by holding the ring, pendant, stone, or coin, and willing the energetic being into place. I also suggest you leave a "back door" for your pooka, allowing it to venture out on its own when resting from its tasks. By doing so, you give your pooka an opportunity to learn, grow, and evolve. Do this by willing it so.

10. Put the ring or pendant on, or carry the stone or coin on your person.

11. If you feel you have made an error in the procedure, release the pooka and try again. To release your pooka, simply merge again as deeply as when you originally created it, and let the pooka go.

12. When you are finished, allow the candle to safely burn down on its own, release the elemental powers, thank deity, and pull up your magic circle. Always carry your pooka with you, calling upon it to perform its tasks when needed. Remember, your pooka reflects or mirrors you, absorbing everything that it comes in contact with it.

Treated with respect, it can become a dear companion. After all, you are its mother and father.

NOW YOU SEE ME, NOW
YOU DON'T, INVISIBILITY SPELL

A computer   A silver candle and holder
Internet service   Paper and pen
A cloak (Please refer to
    chapter 2 for cloak-making
    instructions)

CASTING THE SPELL

Put on your cloak. Then draw a magic circle of silver light around your computer, and call in the elemental powers. Write down the information you want to find out on the Internet on the piece of paper. Fold the paper three times, and put it under the candle holder. Next, light the candle, merge with the flame, and say,

> *Candle light, burning bright*
> *Sacred flame, may I discover*
> *(State what you want to find out on the Internet)*
> *By divine cyber will, so mote it be!*

Now, sit in front of your computer, turn it on, and log onto the Internet. Enter in the URL www.the-cloak.com. Click on "start surfing" and then go to a search engine like Yahoo.com or Dogpile.com. Now you are invisible on the Internet. You can't be seen, you can't be cookied until you gag, and no one can tell which Web sites you have been visiting. When you are done surfing, thank the cyber spirits, bid farewell to the elements, and pull up the circle. Turn off your computer, and allow the candle to burn safely down.

E-MAIL CYBER SPELL

A white candle   E-mail service
A computer

CASTING THE SPELL

Do this spell at midnight. Draw a sacred circle around your computer. Put the candle a safe distance away from your screen, and then light it, dedicating it to your favorite deities. Then turn on your computer, click on your e-mail program, and sit back and merge with the candle flame and screen. Take a few deep breaths to center yourself, and say,

By moonshine the animals sing
By starlight, the owl does wing
Across the window of the Web
Gliding into the timeless ebb.

Oh computer, cyber cauldron of creation,
Weave a brilliant Web for my navigation.
In Internet server and user circles tonight,
Filter out the spam and bring email bright.

I call upon all of my Cyber friends
And invite them to click on now!
I call upon the Cyber Spirits of Earth
And invite them to click on now!
I call upon the Cyber Spirits of Air
And invite them to click on now!
I call upon the Cyber Spirits of Fire
And invite them to click on now!
I call upon the Cyber Spirits of Water
And invite them to click on now!

Oh Great Cyber Goddess keep us whole
Let your power and love fill our souls
Oh Great Cyber God keep us whole
Let your power and love fill our souls.
We are the flow, we are the ebb
We are the weavers of the Internet Web.

Blessed be the Cyber God and Goddess,
Blessed be the providers, servers, and users!
Blessed be all the weavers of the Web
Blessed be! Blessed be! Blessed be!

Now e-mail three people that you know. You can use e-cards to add some visuals to your communication. Just search "e-cards," and you will find a large list to choose from. Next, go to <www.the-cloak.com>, and then surf the Internet for some of your favorite sites on magic. Check out my book, *The Wiccan Web* (with Patricia Telesco, Citadel Press, 2001), for a listing of great sites for witches and wizards. I suggest subscribing to daily news, weather, or joke services, too. These services send you e-mail every day, keeping you current and helping you keep your sense of humor. When you are done surfing, pull up your e-mail and reply to it. Next, thank the cyber Goddess and God, turn off your computer, and pull up your circle. Take the candle into your bedroom, and allow it to burn safely down. As you drift to sleep, repeat silently, "E-mail me." Imagine receiving wonderful e-mail. In the morning, pull up your e-mail again.

FULL MOON DREAM RING RITUAL

A silver candle   Sandalwood incense
A silver or silver-colored ring

Casting the Spell

Cast this spell at midnight on the eve of a full moon. Draw a magic circle of silver light, and call in the elemental powers. Light the candle, dedicating it to a favorite moon goddess. Bathe the ring in the incense smoke for a few minutes, and then place it on the altar in front of the candle. Clear your mind, letting go of all your tensions and worries for a little while. Take a few deep breaths to center yourself, and pick up the ring, holding it in your dominant hand. Hold the ring up toward the North, and say,

> *Helpful Earth spirits of the North,*
> *Empower this magic ring tonight!*

Hold the ring up toward the East, and say,

> *Helpful Air spirits of the East,*
> *Empower this magic ring tonight!*

Hold the ring up toward the South, and say,

> *Helpful Fire spirits of the South,*
> *Empower this magic ring tonight!*

Hold the ring up toward the West, and say,

> *Helpful Water spirits of the West,*
> *Empower this magic ring tonight!*

Hold the ring up to your heart, and say,

> *By spirit, Earth, Air, Fire, and Sea,*
> *With this ring, empower my dreams!*
> *As I will, so shall it be!*

Allow the candle to burn down, and put the ring on a finger of your left hand. As you drift to sleep, repeat silently, "Magic ring empower my dreams."

In the morning, write down what you recall from your dreams, then pull up the circle of silver light, and release the elemental powers. Take off your Full Moon Dream Ring, and place it on your altar. At night, put it back on before you go to sleep to make your dreams magical! For more dream magic spells, please refer to my book, *Dream Magic: Night Spells and Rituals for Love, Prosperity, and Personal Power* (HarperSanFrancisco, 2000).

6

DIVINATION

D IVINATION IS A WAY of invoking and communicating with the Divine. When you use divination, it's like holding a mirror up to yourself and tapping into your Divine nature. In this way, divination tools not only are fortune-telling tools, but also a form of do-it-yourself therapy. It becomes a way to unlock the secrets inside of yourself, helping you move in a more positive direction and attain your magical goals.

Rather than being shrouded in mysticism and a sense of foreboding doom, the art of divination is really all about reading and intuiting life patterns, patterns that move from the past through the present into the future.

Tarot cards, pendulums, dowsing rods, and runes, are some of the tools that can make the task of reading patterns easier, and help you to master the art of divination. At times, the divination tools themselves seem to create the magic involved in divination, but they are only devices that help with the process.

It is you who creates the magic for successful divination. Through practice and experience, you learn to see the magical patterns of your life. These patterns, and their movement through time, is essentially what moves life from the mundane to the magical.

Do you remember what it was like when you first began to read? Words were incomprehensible and looked like some kind of magic scribbling. Then your perspective changed as you learned the letters of the alphabet and how to pronounce them. Then the magic of reading became something you did on a daily basis without even thinking about it. Divination works much the same way.

People from every walk of life all practice forms of divination, the roots of which reach back into the beginnings of humankind, and extend throughout recorded history. In medieval Iceland, "spae-wives" traveled the land foretelling peoples' futures, and in Greece the Oracle of Delphi was renowned for insights into the future.

The idea of knowing the unknown appeals to people as much today as it has in the past. Part of the unknown that divination reveals is within ourselves, which is why divination systems can lead us further on the road to self-exploration and growth. After all, the questions we ask and the answers we seek are very personal.

THE MAGIC OF DIVINATION

An astrologer, scientist, surgeon, and poet, who spoke five languages, Michel Nostradamus was an avid student of the magical arts and one of the greatest wizards of divination. Over four hundred years ago, he foretold the future in writings that have turned out to be remarkably accurate. In one story he is said to have told the lord of a manor that the day's supper would be a black pig. In order to prove Nostradamus wrong, the lord gave explicit instructions to his chef to only cook the white pig. After the supper, the lord delighted in telling Nostradamus that he was wrong in his fortune-telling. Nostradamus held fast to his original prediction, and asked that the chef be called in. When this was done, the chef confessed that when he was preparing the white pig, the dog had pulled it off the kitchen table onto the floor and spoiled it, so he had to cook the black pig.

What this story shows is that divination is all about looking at future patterns, and that sometimes these patterns can't be changed, even when people try to subvert the outcome. This is not to say the future is written in stone or that it cannot be changed. I am simply suggesting that movement through time produces certain life patterns and these patterns have a tendency to move in somewhat predictable ways. People who excel at divination such as Nostradamus have a keen sight into these tendencies. These tendencies figure heavily into the magical arts.

When beginning the study of divination, begin to observe all of things happening in life around you, paying particularly close attention to the way things connect together. This connection is akin to the strands of a spider's web, weaving into one larger fabric. In the popular Christmas movie, *It's A Wonderful Life*, the main character, George Bailey, is given an opportunity to see what life would be without him, and in the process he learns that each person's life is deeply connected with those around them. These connections are one of the things that makes life magical.

After observing the patterns of life for a while, you will begin to see the subtle patterns, those that lay just beyond the obvious patterns that everyone takes for granted. Magic is the practice of noticing and influencing these subtle patterns through expectation, desire, and merging. When you practice magic, you intentionally influence fields of energies, threading and weaving them together in an effort to create positive change and attain your magical goals.

Magic happens when you couple your intention and expectation together with your desire. Intention and expectation plus desire when merged with Divine energy, unleash powerful energies that can be helpful in the art of divination. In addition, the power of your expectation brings forth a force that when unleashed, brings about the outcome you desire.

In Zen Buddhism, there is the concept that you should expect nothing, and in doing so, you become appreciative and thankful for whatever comes into your life. In one way this is a wonderful altruistic concept because it teaches humility, a characteristic that we often lack. In another way by expecting nothing, we are in jeopardy of getting just what we expect—nothing! As actress Lily Tomlin said, "I always wanted to be somebody, I guess I should have been a little more specific."

Your expectations become ingrained and conditioned into your mind, whether positive or negative. They influence your perception of yourself and the outside world. If you expect negative things to happen, then you increase your chances that these negative things will indeed happen, and if you expect positive things to happen, you increase the likelihood that these positive things will come into your life. Don't ever fool yourself into thinking someone else is controlling your life. You are the creator of your reality, and in this role you not only read but intentionally influence the divining process.

YOUR MAGICAL FIELD OF INTENTION

Each one of us emanates a powerhouse of psychic energy, with energy circulating in and out of us in all directions. These fields of energy are called morphogenic fields, and they surround everything. This means that people have an amazing power that they can learn to use for the good of all. This psychic energy has the potential to influence things, and the more focused and congruent a person becomes at gathering and directing this field of energy, the more magical their life becomes.

My son has a Pooh Bear game where the ice cream and balloon cards are like wild cards that move your game piece across the board much faster than other cards. As we play the game, my son chants, "Ice cream, balloon, ice cream, balloon" and then says a few "Abracadabra Kadoos," and he never fails to get one of these two cards, often immediately after chanting its name. Through intention and expectation, together with desire and merging, what he is doing is moving probability way beyond the boundaries of coincidence into the realm of divination. He likes the game because he continually seems to win. He says it's just magic!

Your magical field of intention is a light that emanates from your body. By intentionally extending your energy field, it can create specific magical effects. Your magical field influences a web of change on an energetic level that continues into the physical level. The energetic level is felt in terms of your state of consciousness. The way you think has a great influence on your reality. The physical and energetic constantly interplay and affect one another, so change on one level also influences change on the other level. Change is a by-product of energy and as such moves it around, and these shifts of temporal power and energy can be utilized on many levels in the magic of divination.

Nothing can remain unaffected by what is around it. Everything affects everything else. When doing magic, you need to be aware of your intentions and expectations, and in the process you must take responsibility for your actions. You need to become more aware of how your every expectation affects every aspect of your life and, in turn, the world as a whole.

Every action produces a ripple of effects generated by the original motion. The basic idea in divination is to see the implications in everything. A pattern begins, then moves through time and space, creating ripples that then create more ripples, continuing on into infinity. Reading these ripples or patterns is what divination is all about. By doing this, you inspire your life to move forward, along a path you desire, rather than one that is dictated by someone else. Sometimes these patterns are very subtle and must be intuited. This is why there are so many tools for divination. The tools are meant to put you in touch with these subtle energy patterns.

CRYSTAL SCRYING

Reading the future using a crystal ball is one of the more common forms of divination. Known as crystal scrying or crystallomancy, this method uses crystals as tools for seeing future patterns. Often these crystals are cut in a round shape in order to refract light better.

As with other divination tools, crystals can be used to gain insights into the patterns that are in play all around you. You are the one doing the divining, communicating with the Divine. The crystal is only a tool for helping in the process.

Historically, crystal scryers have occupied positions of importance in the decision-making process of many powerful leaders. Some notables include Merlin the magician, who was often sought by King Arthur because of Merlin's highly developed powers of sight, and the famous seventeenth-century scryer Dr. Dee, who was sought out by Queen Elizabeth I, regarding matters of state.

Down through the ages, witches and wizards have used a variety of reflective surfaces for scrying. By gazing into the light being refracted off a surface, they would see images that gave them insights into life—past, present, and future. In the past in Ireland, Scotland, and Wales, Druid high priests and priestesses used the gemstone beryl to do their scrying. Because of this usage, Scottish Highlanders called these objects, stones of power. In addition, early crystal balls were made from beryl, and only later were they replaced by spheres made from rock crystal.

Native American cultures that traditionally used forms of crystal scrying include both the Indians of the Yucatan, whose diviners placed great reverence on clear stones such as quartz, and the Apache, whose medicine men used crystals for inducing visions.

Scryers were also prominent in the Middle Ages, and in this era were said to have revered their crystal balls. They never allowed their scrying spheres to be exposed to sunlight. They felt that sunlight would hinder the stone's ability to connect and communicate with the psychic mind, an avenue into the Divine infiniteness of Oneness.

If you wanted to learn scrying in the Middle Ages, you had to become an apprentice to someone who was already an accomplished scryer. They taught their scrying knowledge and, many times, passed their scrying crystals on to their apprentices.

Today, crystals are used in communication devices such as radios, telephones, and computers as well as in credit cards, watches, and numerous other technologies. Crystals can be fine-tuned and very exacting when transmitting signals. These are much the same reasons that they work so well in crystal scrying.

The inherent characteristics of crystals are transparency and regularity of patterns, called symmetry. This symmetry makes the crystal act as sort of an antenna, picking up subtle energetic fields. These fields produce patterns of light and shadow which are what the scryer sees.

CRYSTAL SCRYING TECHNIQUE

When doing the following crystal scrying technique, remember to trust your intuition. Your intuition is like a sixth sense that senses things that your other five senses don't. These are the subtle patterns that make divination what it is, the predicting of future events by observing their past and present patterns. The following instructions explain how you can use a crystal for divining your own future.

First, select a stone that is at least thumb size, which refracts light well and feels comfortable to you. It can be a clear crystal point, or a crystal sphere. If you use a sphere, try to get one that is at least as large as a golf ball for scrying.

Once you've chosen your scrying stone, clear it out by pulsating pure white light through it until it is clear. Do this by holding the crystal in your hands, and breathing in deeply. Hold your breath for a few seconds, then pulse your breath out through your nose, not your mouth. As you do this, imagine a bright white light flowing from your hands into the crystal.

The best time for doing scrying is at night, generally the time when the psychic mind is more open. If you don't do your scrying at night, you will need to find a very dark room for your work. Find a quiet spot, and then set up a simple altar, and place the crystal on it. You can use a stand to elevate the stone if you like. Next, place two candles on either side of your crystal. Match the candle color to your scrying goal. For example, if you are scrying to find out about your love life, use red or pink candles. Candles also backlight the stone, making it easier to see images inside of it. If the flame distracts you with its reflections and movements, then try moving the candles until they shine just right on your crystal. If this doesn't work, try using another backlighting source such as a small lamp.

The next step is to relax by breathing deeply for a few moments with your eyes closed. Make an effort to clear your mind of all outside thoughts.

When you open your eyes, take the crystal from the altar and hold it in your hands, feeling your energy moving into it. This is an important step because it connects your energy to that of the crystal. If the crystal begins feeling warm in your hands, it is because it is becoming activated and ready for scrying.

While holding the stone, think about your reasons for wanting to scry. What information are you looking to receive? Career choices, relationships, and life path are three areas that are traditionally explored through crystal scrying. The main thing here is to be clear about your intention and expectation for doing the scrying.

Now put the stone back between the candles, and begin gazing into the crystal, looking deeply into the patterns of light and shadow as they dance around the inclusions and symmetry of the crystal, much like the images in a kaleidoscope. Do this for a minimum of twenty minutes.

Next, move your mind beyond the physical structure of the stone, merging deeper into the light within. The images will trigger impressions and insights within both yourself and the Divine energy you bring forth in your scrying. Practice merging with the crystal for several minutes, until everything flows into one stream of light. This place is where the sight used in divination flows most freely.

After you finish scrying, make a note of the images or messages you received. Clear your crystal by pulsing white light through it a few times, then put your crystal away in a dark place where it won't be exposed to sunlight. I suggest putting a black or dark blue drape over it while you are not using it for scrying. You can snuff the candles, or allow them to burn down on their own.

USING A PENDULUM FOR DIVINATION

When I was younger my parents gave me an oracle game for Christmas one year. Marketed under the name of Kreskin, who was a psychic magician of the time, this game used a pendulum as its main form of psychic exploration. I remember spending hours with my friends, asking questions and receiving answers to questions about love, school, and the future. Some of the predictions came out fairly accurate such as finding my soul mate, having a son, and becoming a writer.

Pendulums come in all types and sizes. Some of them are made with crystals and gemstones such as clear quartz, amethyst, rose quartz, smokey quartz, and citrine. Other pendulums are made of brass, copper, and silver. I have found that the metal pendulums work better for me, but some of my friends like the crystal pendulums better. Pick the one that you like best and one that feels good in your hand.

Be sure to always clear your pendulum before and after use. Do this by pulsing pure light through the pendulum just like you did with your scrying crystal.

Begin by having a clear image of what it is you want to know from the pendulum dowsing process. Many times this image is in the form of a question, such as, "Should I take a new job that has been offered to me?"

Next, on a piece of paper draw a circle with a dot in the middle and put the paper on a flat surface in front of you. Then hold your pendulum in your power hand. Grasp the string at the point where it connects to the stone, and move your thumb and forefinger gradually upward, allowing the pendulum to swing freely. At a certain point, the stone will swing more strongly. Mark this anchor point with a knot. Take your pendulum, and while holding the string at your anchor point, usually about four inches from the crystal, allow the crystal to dangle freely, with its point directly over the dot in the middle of the circle.

Now ask your higher self which point(s) on the circle mean yes. If the crystal moves up and down, then mark the top and bottom of the circle "yes." After this, ask which point(s) are "no," and mark the answer on the circle. This establishes a baseline to work from. If you find you receive the same answer for "yes" and "no," then clear your mind, and try asking again. One of the most important things in this process is to get "the human" or your conscious mind out of the way, until you get a pure connection into the energetic source. Do not move your hand while doing this procedure, but rather hold the tool in one position, allowing it to move on its own.

Once you have marked the circle, ask the question, and notice which way the pendulum moves. The pendulum should give you an answer, in this case, "yes" or "no." Again, if you have problems getting an answer at first, clear your mind and try again.

As you work with pendulums, you will begin to discover what works best for you. You can then expand or modify the technique.

When you are finished using your pendulum, clear it by pulsing it with white light, and then put it away in a special pouch or box for safe keeping.

MAKING A DOWSING OR DIVINING ROD

Dowsing or divining rods have been around for a long time, and are still employed today by certain well drillers to find water. In fact, my neighbor was looking to have a new well drilled because his old one had given out during a fire. He said he had several drillers out who walked the property, and gave him their professional evaluations as to where the well should go. One of the last people to show up was an old man. He snapped a forked stick off a nearby tree as a divining rod, and then walked around the property with the stick pointed out in front of him until he stopped suddenly and proclaimed that spot as the place where the water was. My neighbor, a non-magical, picked up the diving rod and walked over to the same spot, and sure enough when he reached the spot, the stick tugged downward like a magnet as if being magically pulled toward the ground. He drilled fifty feet in that very spot, and now has a well that produces one hundred gallons of water a minute, meaning the driller didn't just hit water, but an underground river.

Besides looking for water, dowsing rods, because of their sensitivity to subtle energetic impulses, can be used for many things including divination. The rods can be made either out of wood or metal. We will be making metal ones, which are more sensitive to energy. You can make these at any time, and even have fun with your family and friends by showing them how use the rods. Keep in mind that it does take a little bit of practice to learn how to work the rods properly. Be patient and enjoy yourself!

You will need two wire coat hangers, two plastic straws, and a pair of wire cutters or pliers.

Begin by cutting the two wire hangers into seventeen-inch sections. Bend the sections into "L" shapes, with the main extending arm measuring twelve inches, and the handle five inches. Cut the plastic straws to fit over the handles in such a way that the extending rod arm swings freely. Bend the bottom ends of the handles slightly to keep the straw securely in place. To make even more sensitive rods, use two seventeen-inch pieces of copper wire in place of the coat hangers, and two five-inch pieces of hollow copper tubing instead of the straws. Copper conducts energy and is much more sensitive.

Once you have assembled your divining rods, hold the handles about waist high, one in each hand, with the rod arms extended straight out in front of you. Take a few deep breaths to calm your mind. Now focus on one of the best experiences you have ever had in your life, something you really liked. The arms of the rods will open outward, demonstrating the power of your positive thoughts and feelings. Next, focus on someone you don't like. Watch how the rods swing inward, and maybe even touch, showing how your energy field contracts inward with negative thoughts and feelings.

Next, select a favorite Divine energy, god or goddess, or spirit guide, and say their name aloud three times. Merge with the Divine energy, and watch how the rods swing wide apart as your energy field expands in response to your positive energy flow.

Then, say a word such as "Hate" or "Pain," and focus on the word, watching how the rods swing inward as your energy field diminishes.

Now you have seen for yourself just how much your thoughts and words affect yourself and others. So make an effort to talk tenderly to yourself and others, using positive words; think loving thoughts. This will empower you.

Your divining rods are also a handy tool when meeting new people and entering new situations. Just find a quiet moment, take a few deep breaths, hold the rods, and say the person's name or state the situation, and watch the rods respond.

You can let others try your rods, and watch how amazed they are at the power of their thoughts and words. Children are especially good at using the rods, and often quickly master the divining process.

RUNE MAGIC

You can purchase runes sets or make them yourself. The rune symbols themselves are living symbols because they represent dynamic forces that are constantly changing and evolving. Traditionally inscribed on talismans, charms, rune rings, and on candles, runes are invaluable in divination, compact, easy to use, and versatile.

Norse magicians known as "vitki" have perfected the use of runes over the last several thousand years. Runes work on several different levels that include the magical and the Divine. Rune masters are well-versed in a variety of rune techniques that they use for divination. The example used in this section is of a three rune pull. This technique is simple but effective, and one that I use on a daily basis.

In early writing systems such the Egyptian hieroglyphics and the Norse runes, the letters had magical meanings as well as literal ones. The runes are one of the few writing systems that kept the magical meanings of the letters intact.

Every rune has three levels to its meaning—the first has to do with the written symbol itself. The seventh rune of the Elder Futhark, which is the oldest form of runes around today, written out looks like the letter "X" in Modern English. The second level has to do with a letter's name and phonetic sound. The seventh rune is named "gebo" and its phonetic sound is that of a "g" in modern English as in the word "good." The third level has to do with a rune's magical or energetic meaning. In the case of "gebo," its magical meaning is the gift. In particular it is the gift of life as given by the Divine. Gebo also has to do with the relationship between the person giving the gift and the person receiving the gift. The point where the two lines of the symbol "X" come together is where the giver and receiver come together as one. Because of this, gebo is often used in love magic.

Norse mythology and stories of creation tell about Odin, the Norse God of wisdom discovering the runes as well as the magical and Divine qualities in each one of them. In divination, the runes tap into an energy that is described in Norse mythology as the three Norns who are named Urd (pronounced urth), Verdandi (pronounced verthanthi), and Skuld (pronounced skulth). They are called the three fates because from their hands come the forces of birth, life, death, and rebirth. Urd begins by spinning the threads of the fabric of life, which she passes on to Verdandi, who then weaves them into their present pattern of existence within the Web of Wyrd, the source of all magic and energetic patterns. Then Verdandi hands the weave to her sister Skuld, who then takes it and unravels it, tossing the strands back into the abyss.

From these three Divine powers, the runes carry a power that allows them to tap into the forces that influence each person's past, present, and future. Each magical pattern has the elements of being created, given life, and coming to an eventual outcome. Again, the runes are the perfect tools for working with these energies.

The following is a listing of runes with their basic qualities of symbol, name, phonetic sound, and divination meaning.

RUNES OF THE ELDER FUTHARK

Name: Fehu, pronounced: fay-hoo
Sound: F
Divination meaning: Wealth and abundance in accordance with the primal forces of creation.

Name: Uruz, pronounced: ooo-ruse
Sound: U
Divination meaning: Static structure, giving form and structure to the primal creativity.

Name: Thurisaz, pronounced: thur-ee-saws
Sound: the unvoiced "th" as in thorn
Divination meaning: Protection, a thorny vine that provides defense against invaders.

Name: Ansuz, pronounced: awn-sooz
Sound: AA (ah)
Divination meaning: Divine knowledge, wisdom, rebirth, creative expression.

Name: Raidho, pronounced: rye-tho
Sound: R
Divination meaning: Represents the solar wagon, circular flow, rhythm, travel.

Name: Kenaz, pronounced: kane-awz
Sound: K
Divination meaning: Knowledge, the internal fire, the guiding light.

Name: Gebo, pronounced: gay-bow
Sound: G
Divination meaning: The Divine gift, exchange, interaction, balance.

Name: Wunjo, pronounced: woon-yo
Sound: W
Divination meaning: Joy, pleasure, hope, kinship, fellowship, wonderment.

Name: Hagalaz, pronounced: haw-ga-laws
Sound: H
Divination meaning: Associated with the Norn Urd, the past, transformation, evolution, merging, harmony, protection.

Name: Naudhiz, pronounced now-these
Sound: N
Divination meaning: Associated with the Norn Verdandi, the need fire, help, resistance, passion, love, shadow self.

Name: Isa, pronounced: ee-saw
Sound: short I
Divination meaning: Associated with the Norn Skuld, ice, slow-moving structure, stasis, delay, gradual integration.

Name: Jera, pronounced: yar-awe
Sound: Y
Divination meaning: Signifies the life cycle and cycle of the Sun, completion, fertility, natural law, progression.

Name: Eihwaz, pronounced: eye-waz
Sound: E and long I
Divination meaning: Symbolic of the yew tree, transcendence, death, rebirth, communication, knowledge, dreaming, magic.

Name: Perthro, pronounced: perth-row
Sound: P
Divination meaning: The turning over of the dice cup, chance, birth, wisdom, luck.

Name: Algiz, pronounced: all-geez
Sound: Z
Divination meaning: A protective force, spirit, sanctuary, refuge, power, divinity.

Name: Sowilo, pronounced: so-wheel-o
Sound: S
Divination meaning: The Divine solar wheel, partnership, power, transformation, understanding.

Name: Tiwaz, pronounced: tea-waz
Sound: T
Divination meaning: Justice, order, victory, loyalty, the mystery of spirituality and faith.

Name: Berkana, pronounced: bur-kan-a
Sound: B
Divination meaning: The Birch goddess, nurturing, rebirth, growth, spirit, concealment, ancestry, transition.

Name: Ehwaz, pronounced: ee-waz
Sound: E
Divination meaning: Duality, twins, nature, movement, partnership, interaction, harmony, traveling to other dimensions.

Name: Mannaz, pronounced: man-nawz
Sound: M
Divination meaning: Represents the "rainbow bridge," moving from this world to the world of the Divine, memory, human, order, intelligence, ancestors, sacred union.

Name: Laguz, pronounced: la-gooz
Sound: L
Divination meaning: Embodies the element of Water, fluidity, life force, birth.

Name: Ingwaz, pronounced: ing-waz
Sound: I
Divination meaning: Embodies the element of Earth, fertility, the seed, energy, gestation, integration.

Name: Dagaz, pronounced: thay-gaz
Sound: hard th
Divination meaning: Embodies the element of Fire, enlightenment, polarity, intuition, well-being, knowledge of the powers of light and dark.

Name: Othala, pronounced: oath-awe-la
Sound: O
Divination meaning: Embodies the element of Air, ancestral connections, prosperity, property, Oneness.

THREE RUNE PULL

Form a question in your mind. What do you want to know? Something about a relationship you have? Something about a choice you need to make? Be clear about what it is you want to know from the runes.

Holding the bag of runes in your hands, breath deeply and feel yourself being filled with a magical power that expands throughout your being. Then imagine that power pouring into the runes in the bag in your hands. Now exhale, feeling all the muscles in your body relax, suddenly being released of any stored feelings of anxiety. In the next breath, feel the power of runes move into your body until you become one with their magic. Each breath draws you further into their Divine power.

Now reach into the bag, and pull out three runes in succession, laying each on the table before you. The first rune gives the background to the question. If your question was about a relationship, then a rune like Isa might mean it's a good idea to move slow, whereas a rune like Wunjo, would mean that you started the relationship out on a successful foundation.

The second rune you pull out has to do with present influences of the question you have asked. In terms of relationship, it is what is happening right now. If you pull Hagalaz, it might mean that things are undergoing major transformation, or if you pull Laguz, it might mean you are really getting in touch with your emotional issues surrounding the relationship.

The third rune represents the future of your question. So if the second rune was Laguz, then the third rune would tell you where this emotionality was moving toward. If you pull Thurisaz, for example, it means you need to be on guard. If you pull Othala, it means you have a chance for Divine love that moves beyond this physical plane.

The longer you use the runes, the more in tune you become with their energies. I suggest you either do a one or three rune pull for each day. Each rune is different, and through experience you will learn their differences. Sometimes rather than predicting the future, the runes tell you something that's inside yourself that you hadn't yet discovered. If you want more in-depth information on the magical uses of runes and how to make your own set, please refer to my book, *The Little Giant Encyclopedia of Runes* (Sterling Publishing, 2000).

THE MAGIC OF TAROT

The very word "tarot" strikes a hidden chord in our hearts. When we first look upon the strange and beautiful cards of a tarot deck, questions immediately come to mind. Where did the cards come from? What is their history? How are they used to divine the future? And what are the meanings of the cards?

These were the same questions I asked over twenty-nine years ago, when I first saw a deck of Rider-Waite tarot cards. During a summer vacation in 1971, I went on a camping and boating trip up the Pacific Coast, from California to British Columbia, with twenty other kids and four camp counselors. One of the camp counselors had a

Rider-Waite tarot deck, and he gave tarot readings to everyone. When it was my turn, he selected the High Priestess for my significator card, and then proceeded to do a basic Celtic Cross tarot spread. I asked him why he chose that particular card as my significator, and he told me it was because he felt the card represented me. I had no idea what he was talking about, but I was so fascinated with the tarot cards, plus the reading was so powerfully accurate that I didn't question him any further about it.

After the reading I asked him to show me how to read the cards, and that's when my powerful friendship with the tarot began. The cards seemed so familiar, like something dear to me that I had left behind with a best friend in another lifetime. I began working with the cards, and to my surprise, it was as if I were a seasoned tarot reader. Everyone started asking me to do readings for them. The results were remarkably accurate.

Over the years, I have cultivated a deep love and respect for the tarot. The cards still never cease to fascinate me, especially now with so many different kinds of tarot decks. In the past five years, my love for the tarot has led to the conception and creation of my own tarot deck, called *The Shapeshifter Tarot*.

The full range and power of the unconscious may never be completely known, but there are ways to explore its landscape. Many tools have been developed for this purpose such as ritual, meditation, visualization, psychotherapy, and dream interpretation. The tarot is another such tool.

Today, tarot reaches far beyond its fortune-telling origins as more people use it as a visual tool for getting in touch with the Divine, and in turn, themselves. No longer considered merely mystical, the tarot is now used primarily for self-exploration. This leads to personal growth and a more enriching life. Words like intuitive and self-exploratory are replacing mystical and occult, to describe the actual experience of tarot readings.

One of the best things about tarot is that everyone can use it. Tarot crosses all spiritual boundaries. You don't have to be a psychic to use the tarot successfully. All you need is the willingness to develop your own natural intuitive abilities. The tarot can help you understand yourself better by teaching you how to tap into your inner resources more confidently and more often. You can use it to connect to your inner source and expand your spiritual awareness.

TAROT ORIGINS

Some witches and wizards say that the tarot came from Babylonia, China, or India. Although their origins are questionable, what we do know about the tarot is around 1370 C.E., a popular fifty-two-card game with four suits appeared in European cities. These cards came from Egypt, and were inscribed with Islamic script and decoration. Europeans then altered the cards to suit their tastes.

In Northern Italy, a fifth suit of permanent twenty-two trumps, which became the Major Arcana, was added to the cards between 1415–1440 C.E. These cards were used in Italy in the fifteenth century as a popular card game with the nobility. Wealthy patrons commissioned unique decks, some of which have survived, the Visconti-Sforza pack being the oldest of these.

For centuries, the most popular version of the tarot was the simple woodcut cards called the *Tarot de Marseille*, which was a French deck derived from a Italian pack of around 1500 C.E. It was this tarot deck that sparked the curiosity and revelation of clergyman, Court de Geberlin, and his collaborator, the Comte de Mellet, that mystical truths were hidden in the cards. These eighteenth-century gentlemen recognized that the images on the cards were more powerful than a simple game would suggest. They connected the cards to Egyptian mysteries and the ancient mystical teaching of Thoth, the Egyptian God of magic and healing.

Later still, the tarot became a representation of the Hebrew Kabbalist teaching, depicting the twenty-two pathways on the Tree of Life. These pursuits continued well into the twentieth century when the tarot was integrated into the practices of several magical traditions, including the Hermetic Order of the Golden Dawn.

A leader of the Golden Dawn, Arthur Edward Waite, is credited with the renaissance of the tarot in the twentieth century. He commissioned artist Pamela Coleman Smith to create what he termed the rectified tarot. Waite was known as a scholar, Christian mystic, and magus. His version of the tarot, called the *Rider-Waite Tarot*, is still used today.

Although the roots of the tarot lay in the mystery traditions, interest in the cards has expanded in the last few decades to include many different perspectives. The new decks reflect these interests. Today's tarot card designs reflect specific trends in mysticism, sexuality, religion, culture, and philosophy. There are hundreds of decks, with more being conceived and created each day. The cards in many of the tarot decks available are deceptively simple, with others being surprisingly rich. Regardless of its design or theme, each tarot card has a role to play in showing how its energy expresses itself the world. Now, with the advent of the Internet, you can get a tarot reading online at the click of your mouse. For example, try www.tarotmagic.com. This gives tarot readers and seekers a tremendous variety of decks and tarot experiences to choose from.

The true test of the tarot through its many shapeshifts is its ability to retain its essential spirit through each incarnation. Regardless of the deck you select and use, the tarot acts as a mirror you can look through to know your many faces and aspects of self. This is what makes each tarot reading such a fascinating and personal experience.

THE MAJOR AND MINOR ARCANAS

Used for centuries to reveal hidden truths, the tarot is basically a deck of seventy-eight picture cards. The standard tarot deck is divided into two sections, the major and minor arcanas. The word *arcana* is the plural of *arcanum*, which means profound secret. To the alchemists of the Middle Ages, the arcanum was the secret of nature. The tarot cards are therefore a collection of the "secrets" that underlie and explain our universe.

The twenty-two cards of the major arcana are the heart of the deck. Each of these cards represents an aspect of our lives. They represent the archetypes, which are evolving patterns of influence that are an inherent part of human nature. In this way, the twenty-two major arcana cards are markers on the path of inner development leading from earliest awareness (card 0, The Fool) to integration and fulfillment (card 21, The World).

Each card in the major arcana has a name and number. Some names convey a card's meaning directly, such as Justice and Strength. Other cards personify a particular approach to life, such as the Magician, High Priestess, or Hermit. Some of the Major Arcana cards have astronomical names such as the Sun, Moon, and Star.

Their archetypical nature gives tarot cards a collective component. Each of us has certain common needs and experiences. The images on the tarot cards capture these universal moments and draw them out. In the form of a Divine picture book that can help awaken your intuition, the tarot has evolved into a collection of the most basic patterns of human thought and emotion. This is why people tend to respond to the cards in similar ways.

While the major arcana expresses universal themes, the minor arcana brings those themes into daily events. These cards represent the activities and feelings that are inherent in daily life. There are fifty-six minor arcana cards which are usually divided into four suits: Wands, Cups, Swords, and Pentacles. The suits are structured similarly to our everyday playing cards with ten numbered cards (Ace–Ten) and four court cards (King, Queen, Knight, and Page). Each suit represents a particular aspect of life and is associated with a specific element. The four tarot suits are as follows:

- Wands—The suit of creativity, action, and movement; associated with the Fire element.

- Cups—The suit of emotions and spiritual experience; associated with the Water element.
- Swords—The suit of intellect, thought, and reason; associated with the Air element.
- Pentacles—The suit of practicality, security, and material concerns; associated with the Earth element.

TAROT READINGS

Most commonly viewed as a tool for gaining insights to life, a traditional tarot reading involves a seeker and a reader. The seeker is the person looking for answers to personal questions, and the reader is the person who knows how to read or interpret the cards. The seeker always mixes the cards while thinking about his or her question, and then cuts the deck. The reader then lays out the cards in a specific pattern called a tarot spread. Each position in the spread has a particular meaning, and each card has its meaning. The reader interprets the blending of these meanings to shed light on the seeker's question. When you read the cards for yourself, you are both the seeker and reader.

Every tarot reading is unique. Readings are the result of a long series of conscious actions. First, you decide to study the tarot; then you select a deck (and there are hundreds to choose from); then you learn how mix and cut the cards, lay out the cards, and interpret the meanings of the cards.

You might be wondering how a deck of cards can possibly tell you anything about anything. Indeed, there are those that think that the tarot is unscientific and merely a plaything at best. I ask that you keep an open mind about tarot and your curiosity piqued. If you are willing to explore the cards and see what they have to offer you, then you are well on the road to successful divination.

Tarot cards have made a real difference in the way I perceive and deal with challenges in my life. They have been extremely helpful when I have faced difficult choices, or when I have been unclear as to which direction to go. I suggest you use the cards for guidance, as a mirror to your inner self, as well as a fortune-telling device. Then, you too will begin to reap the Divine rewards of the mystical treasure of the tarot.

THE FIVE CARD SPREAD

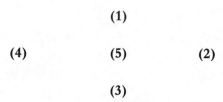

First mix the cards. As you do this, think your question into the cards. Actually imagine putting the question energetically into the body of the cards. After you are done mixing them, cut the cards into three stacks and put them together again into one stack. There are no fast rules on how to mix or cut the cards, so use your intuition and do what feels right.

Take the cards from the top, turning one card over at a time. As shown in the layout above, place the first card above center, the second card to the right of center, the third card below center, the fourth to the left of center, and the fifth card in the center. This five card spread represents the elemental influences of Earth, Air, Fire, Water, and Spirit, that affect the question at hand.

Card #1
This card represents the Earth element, your physical body, surroundings, and environment, and how they influence the question you asked.

Card #2
The second card represents the Air element, symbolizing the intellectual influences in relation to the question. This card reflects your present state of mind.

Card #3

The bottom card represents the Fire element, and indicates the creative forces at work in relation to the question.

Card #4

The fourth card represents the Water element, and reveals your emotions in relation to your question.

Card #5

The center card represents the spiritual influences related to the question at hand, and your connection to the Divine.

There are hundreds of fun and useful ways to use tarot cards. So feel free to use several different decks and reading methods. May all of your divining experiences be helpful and fruitful, propelling you even further into the magical practices of modern witches and wizards.

7

Animal Magic
and Shapeshifting

Because of the cat's natural talent for sensing energies, witches and wizards have traditionally used cats as familiars. In Europe, familiars were attendants to witches and wizards, who could then change their shape into that of the familiar. In Arabia, a familiar was known as a *tabi*, and revealed hidden knowledge to the witch or wizard. Familiars can also be magical creatures such as the phoenix, dragon, or pegasus.

ANIMALS AND THE HUMAN ANIMAL

The relationship between humans and animals is a Divine one. Many magic traditions around the world perceive animals and people as coming from the same Divine place. Because of this connection, the concept of the animal ally as well as shapeshifting into animals, plays an integral part in your magical training. As with familiars, animal allies can be called upon in times of need. To shape shift into an animal is to open a doorway to the inexplicable and mysterious.

Rather than being inferior to us, animals offer a view both of ourselves and the world, a view that moves us far beyond the normal bounds of our perception, often rooted in logic and reason. As shapeshifters, we learn to appreciate life as a sensory experience, moving away from one where life is analyzed and lived as an intellectual process. Trusting our senses as well as our intuition propels us toward our magical goals.

How many times have you had a bad feeling about something, only to have those feelings come true? In the same way, you sometimes have a premonition that something really good is going to happen, and it does. These feelings don't always come true, but still there is something to the ones that do. The trick becomes knowing when they are true and when they aren't. This is why it is important to get in touch with your intuition and understand its nature. It is rooted in everything around you, from the plants and animals to the soil and rocks. Everything is part of the same magic. Nobody knows this more than shamans, who in early tribal societies were the resident magicians. Their job was to know as much as they could about everything, including shapeshifting and animal magic.

THE SHAMAN'S WAY

Based on a true story, the movie *The Emerald Forest* tells of a young boy who is taken and raised by a South American tribe known as the Invisible People. Approaching manhood, the boy goes through a ritual where, under the guidance of the tribal shaman he takes a psychoactive drug, bringing on an experience where he shape shifts into his animal ally, a bird. Later on, when he goes to find help for his tribe, he uses his ability to shape shift into a bird to fly above the city to find the place he is looking for, and the help needed for his tribe.

In tribal societies, the shaman talks with animals, plants, rocks, moon, sun, and stars—with all of creation. In modern society, people rarely communicate with one another, much less the animals, plants, or rocks. As a result, the earth is out of balance and in disharmony. Part of shapeshifting and animal magic is bringing that harmony back into balance by beginning with our own life and moving outward from there. After all, magic begins at home.

Linguistically, the word shaman finds its root in "saman," a word which means "the one who knows." This knowing refers to a particular kind of spiritual healer who communes with the spirit world and uses magical knowledge for healing, divining, and personal empowerment. Shamans can still be found throughout the world.

Probably one of the oldest, if not the oldest form of spirituality practiced by humankind, dating back at least 40,000 years, and perhaps back much further, shamanism is based on an individual's ongoing relationship with the spirits of nature, the elements, ancestral spirits, and other Divine beings such as devas, angels, goddesses, and gods. The shaman's power and knowledge is derived from his or her interaction with these helping spirits, in whatever form they take.

The shaman's way is a lifelong journey, but with a few basic techniques you can experience shamanic or altered states of consciousness such as shapeshifting in just a few minutes. This shamanic altering of your consciousness is a jumping-off point for traveling into the spirit realms, dimensions, and Otherworlds for knowledge and personal empowerment. The key is to build an energetic or spiritual bridge between the magical world of spirits and the world of ordinary reality. As you work with altered states of consciousness more and more, you will find you can change your state of consciousness at will in order to communicate with helping spirits.

Author Hank Wesselman writes in his book, *Medicinemaker* (New York: Bantam Books, 1998), "Seeking connection with the spirits is like shooting an arrow with two points, one that is actually flying in both directions at once. When you reach out to the spirits and they see that the way is open to them, they will enter into relationship with you. Then you will acquire their abilities and their power. You will feel as they feel, see as they see."

The basic techniques of communicating with the spirit world are easy to learn to use, and even beginners can feel stronger and more powerful with their spirit animals by their sides. The journey to the Otherworld of power animal spirits can be facilitated through rhythmic breathing, dancing, chanting, singing, or drumming. Often shamanic practitioners will use a personal spiritual song to produce the shift in consciousness necessary to journey to the spirit world. There are also a large number of cassette tapes and CDs of recorded meditations, drumming, and other music that are specially created to move you into an altered state of consciousness.

All kinds of people, all over the world, are frequently being initiated into shamanic practices spontaneously by the spirits. Contemporary culture refers to these experiences as religious experiences, revelations, out-of-body and astral travel, "A-ha" experiences, psychotic episodes, or waking dreams. Powerful dreams, accidents, or illness can also trigger shifts of consciousness.

The magical reality of the spirit world parallels the ordinary world. Druids trained in Celtic traditions call it the Otherworld. Shamanic practitioners often view the universe and the spirit world as divided into three areas: The Upperworld, the Middleworld, and the Underworld. The practitioner journeys to all three worlds. My experience of journeying to the spirit world and into non-ordinary reality has always been slightly different each time I go there. There are certain experiences, power animals, and beings that are more connected with the Upperworld, Middleworld, or Underworld, but that separation is suggested rather than pronounced. For example, there is a golden eagle spirit that mostly appears in my Upperworld journeys, yet he has also appeared in a couple of my Underworld journeys, where he stands next to a well.

All things have spirit and spirit resides in all things, whether manifested or unmanifested. Universal knowledge becomes attainable as you journey to these experiential and energetic dimensions. I do not suggest you take your body with you on these journeys, yet there are accounts of shamans being able to do just that. My feeling is that there are many things possible that I have not personally seen or experienced, and the evidence supporting cellular shapeshifting is one of those things.

Whether or not the spirit world is real proves to be a moot question once you have journeyed there and made contact with one of

your power animals, ancestors, angels, nature spirits, or the like. Your
perception of reality permanently alters. Time and space suddenly
become responsive to your thought-forms and malleable like model-
ing clay. Because of the extraordinary and supernatural qualities of
shamanic-type experiences, most people radically revise their concepts of reality after journeying to the spirit world. In turn, once you
experience and embrace the otherworlds of spirit, it is not unusual to
have life-changing or spiritual experiences. These spiritual experiences often provide you with an entirely new set of values, behaviors,
and practices. Your field of perception just keeps expanding expo-
nentially together with your magical experiences.

POWER ANIMALS

Some people are born with the ability to understand the speech, communication, and messages of animals. Other people acquire the faculty
as a Divine gift, from a specific power animal, spirit, or by magical
means. Communication with nature opens you up to a storehouse of
knowledge and enables you to do extraordinary things, such as prediction and shapeshifting. Many a folktale begins with the line, "These
things happened long ago, when animals could speak like humans."
That animals can and do speak is an unquestioned fact among Native
Americans in North and South America, among the Australian abo-
rigines, African peoples, in Europe, and the peoples of Asia.

Knowing how to communicate with nature and animals is an
inherent human ability, something we have been doing since the
beginning of our earthly existence. Well-known author of Seneca,
Cherokee, and French descent, Jamie Sams, talks about the ancient
connection between humans and animals in the book *The Mystery of
the Crystal Skulls* (Santa Fe, NM: Bear & Co., 1998) by Chris Morton
and Ceri Thomas: "I will tell you the real story of our creation as I
have heard it from my elders. In the beginning, there was peace on
Earth. . . . There was a golden age when Earth people and animals
could communicate with each other and lived together harmoniously."

She goes on to point out that our earliest ancestors were almost completely vegetarian, meaning they did not eat animals.

In many cultures, myths and legends exist that tell of a time when gods, people, and animals were one. For example, the Egyptian God Souchos was a crocodile himself. In some parts of Africa crocodiles are thought to be the abodes of dead ancestors, and it is said that he who kills a crocodile becomes a crocodile.

Native American tradition says that the Earth is a living woman made by the Old One. After making the Earth Woman, the Old One gathered some of Earth Woman's flesh and rolled it into balls like mud or clay. He made the first group of balls into the ancients. The ancients were people, yet they were also animals. They looked like people, but some walked on all fours. Others could fly like birds, while some could swim like fish. All had the gift of speech, and were more cunning and wise than either animals or people.

Each person's journey and direct communion with the spirits is unique. There is no middle-person, no conveyer of meanings and omens. Your spirit body journeys and directly interacts with other spirits, collecting information and messages of value along the way, information that is provided according to your needs and your ability to comprehend its meaning and purpose. This information can then be applied to everyday life, to help yourself and others.

Time is circular. Keeping this in mind, it means that every living thing now and every thing that has lived or will live on this planet, in the galaxy, and the universe, has a spirit. Spirit is eternal and forever connected to spirit, like an infinite web of light, woven into one, yet with boundless facets.

You are one with your power animals and they are one with you. Everything—spirits, trees, mountains, soil, flowers, dogs, cats, all animals, people, rocks, insects, birds, oceans, rivers, elements, sky, sun, moon, and stars—is connected into one. As William Butler Yeats so aptly wrote, "Though the leaves are many, the root is one." It is up to you to merge with Oneness to alter your state of consciousness, shifting your perception into a more coherent awareness of life.

THE MAGICAL QUALITIES OF ANIMALS

Animals have different magical qualities depending upon the culture. For example, the raven is considered a bird of war and knowledge by the Vikings. Odin, the Norse Father God of wisdom, had a pair of ravens, Hugin (thought) and Munin (memory), that perched on his shoulders. At dawn the ravens explored the Earth and returned at night to whisper the secrets they found in their travels into Odin's ear. In other cultures, the raven is considered a bird of death and a bad omen.

Children are often given a power animal to protect them at night in the form of a stuffed animal: a bear, dog, giraffe, big bird, or a dinosaur, for example. Also, when a child frequently dreams of a certain power animal or is given messages in his or her dreams by power animals, it indicates that the child has shamanic abilities. Often the animal that the child dreams about reflects certain empowering aspects of the child that deserve special attention.

Remember that all animals are your teachers. You are one with nature and animals are your kin; your sisters, brothers, and cousins. For example, ancestor worship in Chinese folklore maintains that people have two souls; the animal soul called the "p'o" and the spirit soul called the "hun."

The destructive buggy whip days of humankind against nature have run their unbalanced course. It is time to wake up to the fact that animals are your equals, not inferior, but at one with the natural world; tailoring their form, thoughts, and behaviors toward survival in their environment. By studying and communicating with animals, you can successfully learn and utilize their many skills and lessons.

Each animal species, just like each plant species, is unique. Beware of the human tendency toward anthromorphism and giving human attributes to animals, instead of letting them be who and what they are. Keep in mind that people are rather tame and conditioned, while animals are wild and less predictable.

Never take the form of an animal to do harm to yourself, other animals, or people. I can't stress this enough in shapeshifting. The whole idea is to experience the animal's knowing and teachings, not to exploit its talents and natural gifts in negative ways.

Modern witches and wizards honor the power of animals and the land, and use their gifts and wisdom wisely. I personally do not condone the use of animals, animal skins, or other animal parts in ritual or spell working at any time. In many magical traditions the altar represents the "living" table of the Divine God and Goddess, and because of its Divine nature, no dead thing is ever laid upon it.

FINDING YOUR POWER ANIMAL

Entering into an altered state of consciousness is the first step to discovering your power animal. Coming in all sizes and shapes, your power animal is the best animal to shape shift with because it mirrors your deepest essence and also reflects qualities and knowledge that you need to survive and progress in the world.

Using visualization, drumming, breathing, and dreaming, you can journey into Otherworlds of experience. During these journeys, you will find that some spirits are helpful and some are not. A key to knowing the difference is paying close attention to the general disposition of the animal's spirit energy. Does it seem friendly or hostile? For example, if you meet with an alligator or other reptile, and it looks like it wants to eat you for dinner, it would be wise to work with another power animal.

Most birds and mammals are benevolent power animals. Also, mythical animals such as the dragon, unicorn, or Pegasus also make powerful animal allies. Go with your intuition and gut feeling.

You may already be aware of your power animal, and that animal may greet you as you journey into other realms, giving you power and assistance. To find your power animal, and to communicate with it once you find it, is a uniquely personal experience. No two people are going to go about it exactly the same way. Some people discover their power animals while dreaming, and others in "A-ha" experiences. Others meet their power animals on spirit journeys, in meditation, and during out-of-the-body experiences.

The simplest way to find your power animal is by paying close attention to animal signs and signals in your daily life. Ways of doing this include noticing what animal names you encounter during the day, what animals you see, what animals are in your dreams, what animals you most resemble, and what animals you admire or think about most. Also be aware of which animals you are most attracted to, and which ones seem to like you. Any behavioral mannerisms you display also give clues to your power animals. For example, do you growl, purr, or flit and fly around a lot? Do you wear clothing with animals on it or drive a car with an animal name such as mustang or jaguar? Noticing all of these little details often provides insights into the larger picture.

When finding your power animal, the locality you live in has a significant impact because the energy and spirits within a particular locale imprint you, and vice versa. Each area has different flora and fauna and this affects the energy of the land. For example, the forests in Northern California are filled with mountain blue jays, squirrels, racoons, foxes, deer, mountain lions, bears, red-tailed hawks, hummingbirds, robins, alligator lizards, and butterflies. Breaking it down even further, Butterflies alone come in such varieties as the Painted Lady, Monarch, and Swallowtail. Making an effort to know and create a bond with the animals in your specific area both helps and empowers you. The best way to create a bond with an animal is to feed it.

TEN-POINT CHECKLIST FOR DISCOVERING YOUR POWER ANIMALS

On a sheet of paper or in a notebook, write down your answers to the following questions. After you finish, review your answers and look for any recurring names of animals or types of animals such as big cats or birds. The animals you have listed either already are, or have the potential to become, your power animals. As such, merging and shapeshifting into these animals can be beneficial and personally empowering.

1. Which animals do you dream about, either while you are sleeping or while daydreaming? Does any particular animal appear regularly in your dreams? If so, which one(s)? Write down the animal you first dreamed about when you were a child. Do you dream about any of your pets, either ones you have now or in the past? Has the memory of any animal dream ever stuck with you for a more than a year? If so, which one(s)?

2. Which animals keep coming into your daily environment? When commuting to work, watching television, shopping, or talking on the phone, which animals keep coming up? Notice the animal signs in people's jewelry, cars, manners of speech, T-shirts, and the like.

3. Determine which animal or animals you most resemble. For example, are you more dog-like, bird-like, or cat-like? Are your movements more like a cat, wolf, lizard, or bird? Ask friends and family members which animal you remind them of or resemble. Many times people will resemble their pets, indicating a close bond between them.

4. Which animals are attracted to you and come up to you? Do cats always come up and rub against you? Do dogs always come over to you and want to be petted? Does your cat or dog sleep with you? Are bees or sea gulls always honing in on you when you are in a group of people? Do deer walk up to you unafraid? Do small birds land in front of you, on your head, shoulders, or hand? The animals that seem to always come up to you are your power animals. They are trying to get your attention by physically interacting with you.

5. Which animals are you attracted and drawn to? When you see an assortment of animal pictures, cards, T-Shirts, or books, which animals most fascinate you? The animals you most resonate with often

make the best power animals. Through time, you will probably be drawn to different animals, depending upon the kinds of energy and wisdom you need at that particular time.

6. Which animals frighten you? Which animals do you run away from? Most people are afraid of one or more animals. Sometimes your fears will take the shapes of the animals you most dread. Confronting these fears through shapeshifting can lead to personal empowerment. Shapeshifting is often a less threatening and more accessible way to become familiar with an animal, rather than interacting with the animal in the flesh. Through shapeshifting, you begin to understand the animals you most fear, and they can then become your allies and potent power animals.

7. Make a note of any animal that has bitten or attacked you in the past. Have you been bitten by a dog, snake, lizard, bird, horse, cat, mosquito, chased by a bull or goat, or been stung by a bee? Traditionally, this means that the power animal is testing your ability to deal with its power. If you survive the attack, you have attained a powerful spirit animal.

8. Which animals do you see most often when you go outdoors? The animals you see and encounter outside in the city and country have helpful messages for you. They teach ways of surviving in their world through their actions and behaviors, ways that can be utilized by people. For example, the squirrel teaches the value of saving for a rainy day, the dog teaches loyalty and tracking ability, while the pigeon teaches homing and directional skills. In addition, by becoming aware of an animal's niche in the ecosystem, it becomes easier to understand where humans fit in.

9. When presented with the opportunity to go to a large aquarium, zoo, animal reserve, or farm, which animals do you focus on? Which animals do you find yourself looking at again and again? For example, I always take the opportunity to ride the elephants when my family visits the zoo, and I spend a lot of time talking with the elephant trainers and patting the elephants. I also spend a lot of time watching the tigers. As you grow older, you will most likely still home

in on the same animals you have for years, but you may also find that you begin to pay more attention to other animals, adding a new favorite or two. This is an indication that these animals have something of value to teach you, something that can help you in daily life.

10. Which animal(s) are you most interested in right now, at this moment, as you read this sentence? Don't so much think about your answer, but feel it. Write down your first response. If the animal you have written down is a power animal you are already aware of, then this animal has more to teach you, especially in the next year. If you have written down an animal that is not already one of your power animals, then spend time becoming familiar with the animal's behaviors, habitat, and other qualities. This animal has great power to offer you if you open yourself up to receiving his/her natural gifts and abilities.

THE BASICS OF SHAPESHIFTING

When you shape shift, you bridge the gap between people, animals, and nature. Bridging this gap allows you access to the many different magical animal energies. With this knowledge, you can release the power of the tiger, a willow tree, or the Earth. This is wisdom that is inherently yours and resides within the coding of your DNA.

As an avenue to connect with your inner nature, shapeshifting is activated by merging with Oneness. Merging is that state of being where the boundaries and separations between everything dissolve away and you see everything as One. At this point, you see the interconnectedness of everything including the relationship between humankind and nature, in particular animals.

When you shape shift, you take on the qualities of the animal you choose to be. Shapeshifting is often done for a limited time and for a particular purpose. With this experience you gain the knowledge you need to continue your magical training.

The first thing in shapeshifting is to choose the animal you want to be. Once you have chosen an animal, such as a dog, you need to spend time merging into the qualities that make that animal unique within the animal world. Observing the animal and becoming familiar with its characteristics and behavior patterns help the shapeshifting process. Direct physical contact with the animal helps in the shapeshifting process. Until you actually touch, or are in close proximity to the animal, it is more difficult to clearly and completely shift and become one with the animal.

When you merge and become one with an animal, you release something inside yourself having to do with your wild nature. People often comment that dogs and their owners are alike, from physical characteristics to the way they act. This is because anyone that is around you for any length of time, picks up your characteristics and you pick up theirs, including animals. This is why when you are starting out, it is easier to shape shift into animals that are within your immediate environment such as a cat or dog.

At first, some individuals have a problem doing shapeshifting because they don't believe they can transform into an animal or any other shape other what they already are. Sometimes getting beyond our conditioned responses is difficult. It is this same conditioning that tells them that magic is not real and that ordinary reality is all that exists.

Belief is not a major factor in the shapeshifting process. The important thing is to let go and start by pretending you can shift into the animal. Allow the animal's energy to flow into you, like a force field that moves both ways, back and forth.

Learning to pretend and have fun with the shapeshifting experience has an immediate positive impact on the results because suddenly you enter a conducive state of mind for shifting forms. When you actually shape shift, you will recognize the experience because your view of reality shifts. Everything from the feel of the earth to your sense of what an animal is becomes altered in a very real way. Every time you shape shift you are awakening some hidden part of yourself.

Ultimately shapeshifting brings humankind closer to nature and animals, to a point where we understand our inherent connection to nature. With every animal that becomes extinct, we lose an inherent part of ourselves. On a very literal and basic level, when we kill endangered animals, we are killing a part of ourselves. The importance of saving species and habitats is crucial to our very existence as they are extensions of our Divine connection to Oneness.

MAGICAL SHAPESHIFTING JOURNEY

Shapeshifting is an expression of your wild nature, and a human skill that has been all but forgotten except by shamans, witches, and wizards. To shape shift into something else is to be privy to the secrets of a state of being where you can feel the inexplicable and mysterious. Human reason does not necessarily apply. Shapeshifting allows for a fuller perspective of life experience. As a way to gather information and build magical skill, it connects you with your creative ability and spiritual center.

Begin by choosing a stone for this journey. Next, draw a magic circle of green light, and then call in the elemental powers. Now sit back or recline comfortably, holding the stone in your receiving hand (left if you are right handed). Take a few deep breaths, relaxing a little more with each breath. Close your eyes, and continue to breathe slowly and rhythmically.

Now imagine yourself sinking into the stone in your hand. Start with your toes, moving up your body, your ankles, calves, knees, hips, stomach, back, arms, neck, and head, sinking even further into the stone. Let all of your muscles go and feel your flesh and bones sink completely into the stone. Merge with the stone and become one with it. Abandon the normal structures of reality, and allow the stone to become fluid and soft, creating a gateway to Oneness, a threshold of awareness. Once you move through that threshold, you are transformed.

Now, in your mind's eye, fully sense the animal you want to shape shift into, before beginning to change shape. Make it an animal that you are very fond of, and see and sense the animal from every angle and move around it in your mind's eye. Imagine yourself becoming that image. For example, if your choice is a cat, say aloud at least nine times,

I am the cat,
The cat is me,
We are one.

See and sense yourself moving like a cat. Imagine laying in the sun grooming your fur, climbing a tree, clawing the carpet, and all the other things cats do. The idea here is to feel yourself becoming a cat, pretending and using your imagination at first if necessary, and paving the way for shapeshifting experiences of being a cat. See, feel, and sense the total experience. Be there completely. Merge and melt into cat-ness, into the other, and become one with the cat. Now take a deep breath, and merge a little deeper. Continue doing this until you can feel the claws coming out of your hands and the whiskers on your face. When you are finished with your shapeshifting journey, thank the animal you shape shifted into, bid farewell to the elements, and pull up the magic circle.

8

DEFENSE AGAINST
THE DARK ARTS

UNFORTUNATELY THERE ARE a few people who use magic to harm others. This practice goes completely against the modern witch and wizard rede that states, "Do what you will, but harm none." Some selfish and hurtful people use magic to manipulate others against their will. They get some sort of demented charge out of watching others suffer. Learning to protect yourself from these mean and nasty people is an important part of your magical training.

In the Harry Potter books, none of the professors who teach the Defense against the Dark Arts class last for more than one school year. This is because it isn't an easy subject to master, particularly when someone is throwing negative magic at you all the time. Some people are overwhelmed and lured by the dark side, finding it hard to resist its seductive power. Others grow weary of the battering of negative energy, give up, and become cynical toward everything. The trick is to defend yourself against the Dark Arts without becoming dark or negative yourself, and without giving in to the dark force.

In the movie *Star Wars*, Darth Vader gives in to the lure of the dark side, and in doing so, does the bidding of the Emperor. Both are horridly ugly, completely self-centered, and particularly cruel. These are not two guys you would want to invite to dinner!

The immediate and short-term benefits of working negative magic may seem at times worth giving in to and becoming part of the darkness, but the long-term effects are never worth the sacrifice. Negativity begets negativity. This negativity caves in on itself. Sometimes it happens instantly, other times it takes a while. Either way, you eventually turn into something foul, evil, and thoroughly repugnant.

You can also develop a certain amount of paranoia and cynicism, which can be justified. However, when it reaches an extreme, it becomes dark in itself, and begins to affect your physical body, mind, and spirit. If you are going to defend yourself against the darkness that sometimes rears its ugly head, it is essential that you remain positive and light-filled, and not draw the darkness into you. When negativity and darkness seem like they are striking from all sides, this advice may seem overly simplistic, but nonetheless keeping your head about you and staying positive is the most important thing you can do to defend yourself against the darkness.

Protecting yourself against the dark side is important whether you practice magic or not. Every day you are bombarded with both positive and negative energy. The positive energy empowers you and the negative energy has the potential of harming you, depending on the power of its intent. To ignore this energy and its effect on your life is extremely naive.

In its simplest form, thought produces a field of energy that is called a magical field of intention or prayer field. With an expectation that is highly directed and focused, this prayer field expands considerably, both in distance and effect. This expansion can either be positive or negative, depending on the energy you direct toward it.

Positivity and negativity are polarities that rather than being on a linear scale to one another, are part of a circular flow that continually changes, propelled by both polarities, much like an electric motor. As the German philosopher Georg Wilhelm Friedrich Hegel (1770–1831) once noted, these polarities combine and their intermingling produces offspring that become combinations of the two, muddying the water as to what is and isn't dark.

The great indicator as to what is dark is how you feel about something. If it makes you feel good and you feel empowered by it, then it is probably light-filled. If it makes you sick, angry, depleted of energy, and nauseous, then it is dark. Rely on your gut feelings and intuition. The idea here is to fine-tune your responses to make them as accurate as you can. Your own finely-tuned feelings can be your greatest ally for identifying the dark side and those that adhere to it.

The dark side works off of fear, anger, and jealousy. Working together, these can be a potently dangerous combination. Eventually the energy of the dark side will deplete and destroy a person. This is the progression of the pattern, and the reason why you can usually spot a negative person a mile away just by their appearance and behavior. If they have chains, daggers, and skulls tattooed or draped over their body, chances are they are not very nice people. You know that. Of course, today some of this kind of decoration is just a taste-less fashion statement geared toward irritating parents!

Trust your feelings and intuition when spotting the dark side, but don't become paranoid in the process. Knowing the difference is the key to improving your life. The differences are often very subtle, but with practice, it is something that you can learn to do well. This knowledge will dramatically improve your life experience.

TRADITIONAL WAYS TO PROTECT YOURSELF

Within traditional magic, some universals exist as ways of defending yourself against the Dark Arts. The magical property of salt is that it neutralizes all negativity. Folklore says that you can bury sage, salt, mullein, or tansy by your front door and it will keep negativity away. Additionally it is said that ferns, marigolds, or lilies, grown near your front entrance or kept as houseplants indoors, will guard your door. This last part is less of a universal and more of a way to make your home more beautiful, and thus making you feel more positive.

Another powerful way to protect yourself, is to chant the names of the goddesses and gods. For example, if you are frightened, you can chant,

Ayea, Ayea, Kerridwen
Ayea, Ayea, Kernunnos
Ayea, Ayea, Ayea!

Keep doing this until your fear diminishes.

In terms of color, a brilliant shade of cobalt blue neutralizes negativity and can be used for general protection. To this end, you can place two crossed iron nails under your doormat and paint your door blue to protect your home from unwanted influences. Also, washing windows with vinegar will not only cleanse them of any unwanted energies, but will also bring blessings into your home.

Using these methods, plus the others covered later in this chapter, will help you learn how to protect yourself energetically from the foul energy of the dark side.

SECRET NAME RITUAL FOR PROTECTION

Names are sacred and can be used as magical tools. The Secret Name ritual is very useful as a means for protection against any negative or dark magic attack. The idea is to merge with Oneness and discover a special name for yourself, a name that has always been your name.

Your Secret Name arises from Divine creation, a point where you can see anything and find everything. Over and over again, speak aloud to yourself, preferably someplace where no one else can hear you. Address your essence and ask your inner self to reveal your secret name. Often many names will fill your mind, making it hard to find your secret name. The important thing is to hone in on the one name that keeps coming up.

Use your dreams as a device for finding your secret name. Before going to sleep at night, give yourself the suggestion that will discover your secret name in your dreams. Also, give yourself the suggestion to remember your secret name in the morning when you wake up. Do this until you receive a name that seems right to you.

It might take a day, week, or a couple of months to find the right secret name. When you do, you should have no doubt that it is your true secret name. Intuition is an important ingredient in this process. Never, and I do mean NEVER tell anyone your secret name, and never, again I mean NEVER write it down on anything. There are absolutely no exceptions!

When you do find your name, it is time to do the secret name ritual in order to strengthen your secret name's magical protective power. Do this ritual in private, making sure no one can hear you.

Begin by stating the name, and then say that all the previous names you have been known by are not your true names. Only one name represents the true you, and that is your secret name. Then say the name three times,

> *My secret and true name is (insert name).*

Once you have done this, then say,

> *No one can harm me with any negative work of magic*
> *Unless they know my secret and true name.*

Again, say your secret name aloud three times,

> *My secret and true name is (insert name).*

Next, create an eternity clause in your secret name ritual. Do this by setting up impossible tasks that anyone finding out your secret name and wanting to do you harm, would have to do before being able to harm you with their dark magic. For example, say,

> *Before anyone can use my Secret Name against me,*
> *They must count all the atoms, one by one,*
> *Of all of the celestial bodies of the cosmos*
> *Over and over again, backwards and forwards,*
> *Forever and a day. So be it!*

When you are done, repeat the whole process a minimum of three times. Every time you do your secret name ritual, you reinforce a pattern or shield of strength, protecting yourself from negativity. Remember: Never, never write down your secret name or tell anyone what it is.

After you finish your secret name ritual, you may feel a little strange, sort of like a different person. This is a normal side effect of the ritual. When you correctly do the ritual, in essence you become a new person with a new name. Your secret name becomes a powerful ally and shields you from the Dark Arts, no matter what form they take. Whenever you feel as though you are under attack, just silently repeat your secret name until the attack stops.

DREAM KNIGHT PROTECTION RITUAL

All of us, at one time or another, could use our very own Knight Errant to keep us from harm and attack. This ritual helps you to establish communication with your Knight Protector, for purposes of protection and guidance. Do this ritual preferably on a Sunday, Tuesday, or Thursday night, on or just before the full moon. Allow about one hour for completing this three-part ritual, which blends a ritual bath, candle magic, and the ancient magical art of scrying into one.

You will need the following ingredients:

A warm bath
3 pinches of thyme
3 lemon slices
Jasmine oil
3 white candles and holders and 3 blue candles and holders
A clear glass filled with water
Sandalwood incense and a censor
A ballpoint pen or quill

Begin by taking a warm bath and adding the thyme, lemon slices, and three drops of jasmine oil to the water. Soak for at least ten

DEFENSE AGAINST THE DARK ARTS

minutes. As you bathe, breathe deeply by inhaling for three counts, holding your breath to the count of three, and then exhaling completely. As you do this, imagine a protective egg of white light surrounding you.

As you soak in your magical bath, take a few minutes to decide what you would like to ask your Dream Knight when you meet him or her. Is there someone or something you need your Dream Knight to protect you from? Make a mental note of the things you would like to say when you meet. I also suggest you jot down a few questions or ideas for your Dream Knight as soon as you get out of the bathtub. Put your notes on your altar where you can refer to them. Dip the six candles into the bath water before draining it. Dry the candles, and then place them on your altar, along with the pen, and a clear glass of water.

Next, draw a magic circle of blue-white light, call in the elemental powers, and light the incense. Focus on the purpose of the ritual, and state your intent and expectation,

> *I am here tonight to make contact with,*
> *And gain protection from my Dream Knight.*

Then use the pen or quill to inscribe the words "Dream Knight" on the first blue candle. Next, apply a thin film of jasmine oil on the candle body, and put it in its holder on the altar. Wipe the oil off your hands, and light the candle. Merge with the candle flame, and say,

> *May this candlelight stretch beyond*
> *Across the celestial realms to all worlds.*
> *Creating a path of light for my Dream Knight,*
> *To come now and protect me tonight.*

Use the pen or quill to inscribe words, "Dream Knight" on the second blue candle, and then apply jasmine oil to the candle body.

Place the candle in its holder, and wipe the oil from your hands.
Merge with the candle flame, say,

> *May this spirit light reach beyond*
> *Across the celestial realms to all worlds.*
> *Building a bridge of light for my Dream Knight*
> *To cross now and protect me tonight.*

Inscribe the same words, "Dream Knight," on the third blue candle,
once again applying oil to the candle body, and putting the candle in
its holder on the altar. Wipe the oil off your hands, light the candle,
and merging with the flame, say,

> *May these three lights shine beyond*
> *Across the celestial realms to all worlds.*
> *Weaving a thread of light for my Dream Knight*
> *To follow now and protect me tonight.*

Next, inscribe the word "Protection" on the three white candles, and
dress them with jasmine oil. Place them in their holders, positioning
them in front of the three blue candles. Wipe your hands, and then
light the white candles, one at a time. As you do, merge with each
flame, and say,

> *May this spirit flame burn true*
> *Dream Knight now let me see you!*

Position the clear glass of water in the middle of the candles, and sit
or recline comfortably. Gaze into the glass of water, while chanting
the words "Dream Knight," over and over. Just keep gazing at the
water, blinking naturally, and remaining focused on the glass. Allow
whatever images or sensations to occur in the water. Eventually a
misty shadow, figure, or face will appear in the water. The image usually appears within a few minutes to about twenty-five minutes.
When a shape appears, ask the image if he or she is your Dream
Knight. You will sense an answer. If the answer is yes, proceed with

your request or questions. If it's not, then stop the ritual, and pull up the circle and try again another night. If the answer is yes, proceed with your request or questions. Then ask your Dream Knight to return when you call him or her by name. When you are finished communicating, thank your Dream Knight, and make a note of any answers or messages you receive. Allow the candles to burn safely down, or snuff them out. As you drift to sleep, repeat silently,

> *Dream Knight protect me.*
> *So be it, blessed be!*

Know that your Dream Knight is always there to protect and guide you, especially in your sleep.

In the morning, drink the glass of water, write down what you recall of your dreams, bid farewell to the elemental powers, and pull up the circle.

CREATING AN AMULET FOR PROTECTION

People traditionally wore amulets as protective charms, usually in the form of a necklace or ring. They were also hung in the house, and used to repel or drive away harmful energies. Traditionally made of metal or stone, amulets are similar to talismans, but differ in that amulets specifically contain protective powers. Throughout history, amulets have been made by alchemists, witches, shamans, and priests, and sold or given to people wanting to protect themselves against violence, illness, thieves, and bad luck. Worn by queens and kings, popes, diplomats, merchants, and nearly everyone else, amulets appeal to the part of human nature that puts trust in certain lucky objects. You probably already have some kind of amulet, or little object, in your car, at home, or on your person, that has a special meaning to you.

You can create your own amethyst amulet to use for protection. Amulets made of gemstones, such as amethyst, have always been valued more highly than those made from other materials. Amethyst has a reputation for its protective, healing, and spiritual powers. When worn, it protects you against the dark side. The best time for creating this amulet is on a full moon.

To make this protection amulet you will need:

A small piece of tumbled amethyst to act as the amulet itself
Cedar incense and censer
A purple candle
A white candle
A blue candle
A ballpoint pen
Lavender oil

Begin making your amulet by washing the candles in cool salt water, drying them, and then placing them on the altar with the other ingredients. Next, draw a magic circle of lavender-purple light, and call in the elemental powers. Then light the incense, dedicating it to a protective god or goddess, for example Tyr, the Norse God of battle and justice. In mythology, he sacrifices his hand in order to protect Asgard, the home of the Gods, from the evil and destructive power of the gigantic Fenris Wolf.

Use the pen to inscribe the words "Protection From Darkness" on each of the candles, and then dress them by rubbing lavender oil on them. Lavender promotes protection and clarity of thought. Place the candles in their holders on the altar in a triangular configuration. Rub three drops of oil over the amethyst, and then position the stone in the middle of the triangle. Wipe the oil off of your hands, and light the candles, dedicating each one to the protector god or goddess you have chosen to help you.

Next, face the altar and focus all of your attention on the amethyst stone. Merge with Oneness, and fill your mind with protective power. Imagine everything that means protection to you, for example, a locked door, a favorite god or goddess, your family, an energy shield, or a large dog.

Now pick up the stone, and holding it between your palms, use deep rhythmic breathing to breathe your feelings and thoughts of protection directly into the amethyst. See and sense your mind energy being absorbed by the stone. Merge with the stone, and say three times,

> *(Insert name of the goddess or god), bestow into this stone,*
> *The power to repel all invaders,*
> *Protect me in waking and in dream*
> *Hear me now, so mote it be!*

Put the stone back on the altar, in the middle of the candle triangle, and clap your hands three times. Allow the candles to safely burn down as you drift off to sleep. In the morning, bid farewell to the elemental powers, and pull up the circle.

Carry your amethyst amulet on your person during the day, and at night put it inside your pillowcase while you sleep. Each week, put three drops of lavender oil on your amulet to reinforce its protective powers.

MAKING A PROTECTIVE CHARM

Using St. John's Wort, a traditional herb used for banishing negativity, this protective charm is great for warding off illness, while in the process, increasing your courage and willpower. You can hang St. John's Wort in your bedroom to prevent nightmares and to protect you from negative powers. Make this charm on a waning moon, preferably on a Sunday or Tuesday night.

You will need:

A large bowl
A 9-inch by 9-inch white cotton cloth
An 18-inch length of purple ribbon or yarn
1 oz. ground cumin
1 lb. sea salt

9 bay leaves
9 pinches of St. John's Wort
9 pinches dried rosemary
9 whole cloves

At dusk, just before it gets dark, mix the sea salt and ground cumin together in the large bowl, and take it outside. Begin at the end of your driveway (or the entryway to your home such as a stairwell or walkway). Face East and then walk completely around your property in a clockwise pattern, sprinkling the herbal mixture in the bowl along the edges of your property, ending at the same point you began. Imagine a protective border of white light coming from the herbs. The salt and cumin keep unwanted energies from entering your property. The cumin can be irritating to your eyes, nose, lips, and so forth, so be careful.

Go back indoors and wash the herbs off your hands, and then mix the other herbs together, piling them in the center of the white cloth. Bring each corner of the cloth up to the center, one at a time, in a clockwise motion, beginning with the topmost (North) corner. When all of the corners are together, four folds will be sticking out. In a clockwise motion, bring the corners of these folds into the center as well. Use the purple ribbon or yarn to wrap around the neck of the cloth nine times, just above the herbs, holding them in place. Each time you wrap the ribbon around say,

> *Three and three and three is nine*
> *Each wrap makes this charm divine.*
> *Blessed be! So be it!*

Then, knot each end of the ribbon nine times. With each knot you tie, say,

> *Three and three and three is nine*
> *Each knot makes this charm divine.*
> *Blessed be! So be it!*

Lie back, and hold the charm in your hands. Close your eyes, and imagine a warm white light completely surrounding you like a brilliant white egg. See and sense this white light moving through your arms, hands, and into the charm bag. Feel the warmth, the safety, the protection of this bright white light. Imagine the charm bag radiating a brilliant light, and then merge completely with the light. Hold the charm in your hands as you sleep, or place it in your pillowcase for the night. I suggest that you empower the charm every week or so, making a new charm bag once a month, until you feel safe and protected from negative energies.

9

CONTINUING YOUR WITCH AND WIZARD TRAINING

THIS TRAINING GUIDE HAS provided you with a basic view into the world of the magic. How deeply rooted you are into the non-magical world has a lot to do with how well you fared. Like any art and craft, magic takes a certain discipline when learning and gets easier the more you practice it.

Whether you come from a magical or non-magical upbringing, the important thing is how you use the training both in this and some of the other books listed in the bibliography as you progress from here. Again, it is all a matter of your intention and expectation.

Where you go from here in terms of your magical training is up to you and depends on your choices. You could learn a Mystery Tradition. There are many that have teachings that will help you hone your magical abilities. The other way is to become proficient in a variety of subjects, blending them together into something that is your own. Whatever path you choose is up to you.

One thing everyone can do is to continue to believe in the existence of magic. Always bring as much magic into your life as possible. Remember when things start getting crazy, think about what Rudyard Kipling wrote, "Don't lose your head when all about you are losing theirs." Rudyard Kipling was a magician of words and this is one of the keys when learning magic.

Expect magic in your life, and it will happen, even when all hope seems lost. This is truly what life is about. There is a story about a little girl who is told her little brother is going to die without a miracle. She goes to the drug store and asked how much a miracle costs, she only has $1.37 from her piggy bank. After the druggist tries to get rid of the little girl, telling her they don't sell miracles, a man at the counter speaks up and tells the girl that today, miracles cost only $1.37. The man just happened to be a brain surgeon at a prestigious hospital, and when he heard her story he gave the little girl's brother the operation he needed.

Magic happens, often in many forms. Never give up hope. Positive expectation is often what propels the self and humanity forward into a better future. Simply put, magic is the belief in something beyond mundane reality as it stands now. Magic is a belief in the future; a hope that it can be better than the past.

There has always been a battle of polarities—good and evil—that has been going on from the past to the future, and that seems to continue. Always have a clear expectation of what you want to have happen in your life, otherwise you open yourself up to random forces of chaos. Failing to have intention in your life is like intending to fail. In terms of sailing, your intention is your rudder. Without it, you have no say as to where you are going. Eventually your boat floats aimlessly in circles. Around and around you go, where you stop and move forward nobody knows. You just drift aimlessly around and around for eternity. At best, it will make you dizzy, but it won't help you attain your magical goals.

If you set your sights on where you want to go, you greatly increase your chances of reaching your destination, whether in the magical or non-magical world. You must accept and take responsibility for your every action if you expect to become an expert witch or wizard. There is no blame, only responsibility.

Stay resilient, no matter what the odds. Life often leaves many scars, and from these we hopefully learn to become better human beings. Sometimes things work for us and sometimes things work against us. Knowing the difference is essential not only to magic, but life itself.

Life often swings within us from one polarity to the next, until we find some balance between these extremities. At times it is painful, but without the polarities we would no doubt be blobs upon the concrete, without motivation or direction. The polarities are what give us motivation that in turn provides the magical expectation. Without it, life goes nowhere.

Life at times can be a dragon spitting fire in your face and at other times it is a symphony of birds in the forest with the luminescence of positivity in full force. Ultimately, it all comes down to perspective. How you view your life is much how your life is—the choice is yours. You can make life wonderful or you can make it a burden. The choice is yours.

We are all assailed by the outside world to the point where we become cautious about everything we do. On one hand caution is a good characteristic for survival in the modern world, but on the other hand, it can cut us off from the world around us and the ones we love. There is a world out there that is as ugly as any nightmare you could ever imagine, and then there is a world out there that is greater than the best fantasy that you could ever envision. From these two diversities, we create a world that is both cruel and wonderful. The idea in positive magic making is that the wonderful nature of life prevails, and that people be kind to each other not only at Christmas, but all year long. That's what makes life truly magical.

BIBLIOGRAPHY

Alexander, Skye. *Magickal Astrology.* Franklin Lakes, NJ: New Page Books, 2000.

Andrews, Ted. *Animal Speak.* St. Paul, MN: Llewellyn Publications, 1993.

Beyerl, Paul. *A Compendium of Herbal Magic.* Custer, WA: Phoenix Publishing, Inc., 1998.

Blair, Nancy. *Amulets of the Goddess.* Oakland, CA: Wingbow Press, 1993.

Bonwick, James. *Irish Druids and Old Irish Religions.* New York: Dorset, 1986.

Bord, Janet and Bord, Colin. *Mysterious Britain.* London: Paladin Books, 1974.

Bowater, Margaret M. *Dreams and Visions: Language of the Spirit.* Freedom, CA: Crossing Press, 1999.

Bowes, Susan. *Notions and Potions.* New York: Sterling Publishing Co., Inc., 1997.

Bulfinch, Thomas. *Bulfinch's Mythology.* Garden City, NY: Garden City Publishing Co., Inc., 1938.

Campbell, Joseph. *The Power of Myth.* New York: Doubleday, 1988.

Castaneda, Carlos. *The Art of Dreaming.* New York: HarperCollins, 1993.

Ceram, C. W. *Gods, Graves, and Scholars.* New York: Bantam Books, 1972.

Creasy, Rosalind. *The Edible Herb Garden.* Boston: Periplus Editions, 1999.

Cunningham, Scott. *The Complete Book of Incense, Oils, and Brews.* St. Paul, MN: Llewellyn Publications, 1989.

Cunningham, Scott. *Encyclopedia of Magical Herbs.* St. Paul, MN: Llewellyn Publications, 1985.

Cunningham, Scott. *Living Wicca.* St. Paul, MN: Llewellyn Publications, 1993.

Devereax, Paul and Devereax, Charla. *The Lucid Dreaming Kit.* Boston: Tuttle/Journey Editions, 1998.

Drew, A. J. *Wicca for Men.* New York: Citadel Press, 1998.

Dunwich, Gerina. *Wicca A to Z.* New York: Citidel Press, 1997.

Evans-Wentz, W. Y. *The Fairy Faith in Celtic Countries.* New York: Citadel Press, 1990.

Farrar, Janet and Stewart. *A Witches' Bible Compleat.* New York: Magical Childe, 1984.

Farrar, Stewart. *What Witches Do.* London: Peter Davis Limited, 1971.

Ford, Patrick K., translator. *The Mabinogi and Other Medieval Welsh Tales.* Los Angeles: University of California Press, 1977.

Gannon, Linda. *Creating Fairy Garden Fragrances.* Pownal, VT: Storey Books, 1998.

Gimbutas, Marija. *The Language of the Goddess.* San Francisco: Harper & Row, 1989.

Gimbutas, Marija. *The Goddesses and Gods of Old Europe.* Berkeley, CA: University of California Press, 1982.

Godwin, Malcolm. *The Lucid Dreamer.* New York: Simon & Schuster, 1994.

Goldstein, Nikki. *Essential Energy: A Guide to Aromatherapy and Essential Oils.* New York: Warner Books, 1997.

Grabhorn, Lynn. *Excuse Me, Your Life Is Waiting.* Seattle, WA: Hara Publishing, 1999.

Green, Miranda J. *Dictionary of Celtic Myth and Legend.* New York: Thames and Hudson, 1997.

Grimal, Pierre (ed.). *Larousse World Mythology.* London: Paul Hamlyn, 1965.

Harner, Michael. *The Way of the Shaman.* New York: Bantam, 1986.

Heath, Maya. *Cerridwen's Handbook of Incense, Oils, and Candles.* San Antonio, TX: Words of Wizdom International, Inc., 1996.

Hopman, Ellen Evert. *A Druid's Herbal for the Sacred Earth Year.* Rochester, NY: Destiny Books, 1995.

Jacobs, Joseph. *Celtic Fairytales.* New York: Dover Publications, Inc., 1968.

Jung, Carl G. *The Archetypes of the Collective Unconscious.* Princeton, NJ: Princeton University Press, 1990.

Keville, Kathi, and Green, Mindy. *Aromatherapy: A Complete Guide to the Healing Arts.* Freedom, CA: Crossing Press, 1995.

Knight, Sirona. *Celtic Traditions.* New York: Citadel Press, 2000.

Knight, Sirona. *Dream Magic: Night Spells and Rituals for Love, Prosperity, and Personal Power.* San Francisco: HarperSanFrancisco, 2000.

Knight, Sirona. *Exploring Celtic Druidism.* Franklin Lakes, NJ: New Page Books, 2001.

Knight, Sirona. *Greenfire: Making Love With the Goddess.* St. Paul, MN: Llewellyn Publications, 1995.

Knight, Sirona. *The Little Giant Encyclopedia of Runes.* New York: Sterling Publishing Co., 2000.

Knight, Sirona. *Love, Sex, and Magick.* New York: Citadel Press, 1999.

Knight, Sirona. *Moonflower: Erotic Dreaming With the Goddess.* St. Paul, MN: Llewellyn Publications, 1996.

Knight, Sirona. *The Pocket Guide to Celtic Spirituality*. Freedom, CA: Crossing Press, 1998.

Knight, Sirona. *The Pocket Guide to Crystals and Gemstones*. Freedom, CA: Crossing Press, 1998.

Knight, Sirona, et al. *The Shapeshifter Tarot*. St. Paul, MN: Llewellyn Publications, 1998.

Knight, Sirona, and Telesco, Patricia. *The Wiccan Web*. New York: Citadel Press, 2001.

Leach, Maria, Editor. *Standard Dictionary of Folklore, Mythology, and Legend*. New York: Funk & Wagnalls Co., 1950.

LeBerge, Stephen. *Lucid Dreaming: The Power of Being Awake and Aware in Your Dreams*. Los Angeles: Jeremy P. Tarcher, Inc., 1985.

Linn, Denise. *The Secret Language of Signs*. New York: Ballantine Books, 1996.

Long, Jim. *Making Herbal Dream Pillows*. Pownal, VT: Storey Books, 1998.

Malory, Sir Thomas. *Le Morte D'Arthur, Vols. I & II*. New York: Mentor Classics, 1962.

Markale, Jean. *The Druids*. Rochester, VT: Inner Traditions, 1999.

Markale, Jean. *Merlin: Priest of Nature*. Rochester, VT: Inner Traditions, 1995.

Monaghan, Patricia. *The Book of Goddesses and Heroines*. St Paul, MN: Llewellyn Publications, 1990.

Mormouth, Geoffrey. *History of the Kings of Britain*. New York: E.P. Dutton & Co., 1958.

Morrison, Dorothy. *Everyday Magic*. St Paul, MN: Llewellyn Publications, 1998.

Morton, Chris and Ceri Thomas. *The Mystery of the Crystal Skulls*. Santa Fe, NM: Bean & Co., 1998.

Nahmad, Claire. *Cat Spells*. New York: Random House, 1998.

Pajeon, Kala and Ketz. *The Candle Magick Workbook*. New York: Citadel Press, 1991.

Paterson, Helena. *Handbook of Celtic Astrology*. St. Paul, MN: Llewellyn Publications, 1995.

Rector-Page, Linda. *Healthy Healing*. Sonoma, CA: Healthy Healing Publications, 1992.

Ross, Anne. *Pagan Celtic Britain*. New York: Columbia University Press, 1967.

Rowling, J. K. *Harry Potter and the Sorcerer's Stone*. New York: Scholastic, Inc., 1997.

Rowling, J. K. *Harry Potter and the Chamber of Secrets*. New York: Scholastic, Inc., 1999.

Rowling, J. K. *Harry Potter and the Prisoner of Azkaban.* New York: Scholastic, Inc., 1999.

Rowling, J. K. *Harry Potter and the Goblet of Fire.* New York: Scholastic, Inc., 2000.

Ryall, Rhiannon. *West Country Wicca.* Custer, WA: Phoenix Publishing Co, 1989.

Sabrina, Lady. *The Witch's Master Grimoire.* Franklin Lakes, NJ: New Page Books, 2001.

Serure, Pamela. *The 3-Day Energy Fast.* New York: HarperCollins, 1997.

Silver, Helene. *Rejuvenate.* Freedom, CA: Crossing Press, 1998.

Sitchin, Zecharia. *When Time Began.* Santa Fe, NM: Bear and Company, 1993.

Squire, Charles. *Celtic Myth and Legend.* Franklin Lakes, NJ: New Page Books, 2001.

Starhawk. *The Spiral Dance.* San Francisco: HarperSanFrancisco, 1979.

Stewart, R. J. *Celtic Gods, Celtic Goddesses.* New York: Sterling Publishing Co., 1990.

Stewart, R. J. *The Living World of Faery.* Glastonbury, Somerset: Gothic Image Publication, 1995.

Stewart, R. J. *The Power Within the Land.* Rockport, MA: Element Books, 1992.

Telesco, Patricia. *A Charmed Life.* Franklin Lakes, NJ: New Page Books, 2000.

Telesco, Patricia. *Spinning Spells, Weaving Wonders.* Freedom, CA: Crossing Press, Inc., 1996.

Tierra, Lesley. *The Herbs of Life.* Freedom: CA: Crossing Press, 1992.

Valiente, Doreen. *The Rebirth of Witchcraft.* London: Robert Hale, 1989.

Valiente, Doreen. *Witchcraft for Tomorrow.* New York: St. Martin's Press, 1978.

Weinstein, Marion. *Earth Magic.* New York: Earth Magic Productions, 1998.

Wesselman, Hank. *Medicinemaker.* New York: Bantam Books, 1998.

Wilde, Lady. *Ancient Legends, Mystic Charms and Superstitions of Ireland.* New York: Lemma Publishing, 1973.

Worwood, Valerie. *The Complete Book of Essential Oils and Aromatherapy.* New York: New World Library, 1995.

Yeats, W. B. (ed.). *Fairy and Folk Tales of Ireland.* New York: Macmillan Publishing Co., 1983.